60 Casserole Recipes for Home

By: Kelly Johnson

Table of Contents

Appetizers:

- Classic Beef and Potato Casserole
- Chicken Alfredo Bake
- Vegetarian Lasagna Casserole
- Tuna Noodle Casserole
- Broccoli and Cheese Chicken Casserole
- Mexican Taco Casserole
- Eggplant Parmesan Bake
- Shepherd's Pie
- Spinach and Artichoke Chicken Casserole
- Sausage and Mushroom Breakfast Casserole
- Sweet Potato and Black Bean Enchilada Casserole
- Chicken and Rice Casserole
- Zucchini and Tomato Gratin
- Buffalo Chicken Mac and Cheese Bake
- Mediterranean Quinoa Casserole
- Turkey Tetrazzini
- Ratatouille Bake
- BBQ Pulled Pork Mac and Cheese
- Creamy Mushroom and Wild Rice Casserole
- Shrimp and Grits Casserole
- Italian Sausage and Peppers Bake
- Caprese Pasta Bake
- Green Bean Casserole
- Lemon Garlic Chicken and Rice Casserole
- Beef and Broccoli Quinoa Bake
- Chicken Enchilada Casserole
- Cajun Jambalaya Casserole
- Artichoke and Spinach Dip Chicken Bake
- Cheesy Hash Brown Casserole
- Egg and Sausage Breakfast Bake
- Pesto Chicken and Penne Casserole
- Creamy Corn and Bacon Casserole
- Hawaiian Pizza Casserole

- Turkey and Cranberry Stuffing Casserole
- Baked Ziti with Meatballs
- Brussels Sprouts and Bacon Gratin
- Chicken Cordon Bleu Casserole
- Butternut Squash and Sage Lasagna
- Chili Cornbread Casserole
- Greek Moussaka
- Philly Cheesesteak Casserole
- Creamy Chicken and Mushroom Casserole
- Sloppy Joe Tater Tot Casserole
- Three-Cheese Baked Ziti
- Cabbage Roll Casserole
- Crab and Artichoke Casserole
- Teriyaki Chicken and Rice Casserole
- Quinoa and Black Bean Enchilada Bake
- Pumpkin Mac and Cheese
- Bacon and Potato Breakfast Casserole
- Chicken Pot Pie Casserole
- Tex-Mex Layered Bean Dip Bake
- Sausage and Spinach Strata
- Lemon Blueberry French Toast Bake
- Tomato Basil Quinoa Bake
- Chicken and Dumplings Casserole
- Mediterranean Eggplant and Chickpea Bake
- Ham and Swiss Croissant Casserole
- Buffalo Cauliflower Mac and Cheese
- Cornbread and Sausage Stuffing Casserole

Classic Beef and Potato Casserole

Ingredients:

- 1 1/2 pounds ground beef
- 1 onion, finely chopped
- 2 cloves garlic, minced
- 1 cup frozen peas
- 1 cup carrots, diced
- 1 can (10.75 ounces) condensed cream of mushroom soup
- 1/2 cup beef broth
- Salt and pepper to taste
- 4 cups potatoes, peeled and thinly sliced
- 1 1/2 cups shredded cheddar cheese
- Fresh parsley, chopped (for garnish)

Instructions:

Preheat your oven to 375°F (190°C). Grease a 9x13-inch baking dish.
In a large skillet, brown the ground beef over medium heat until fully cooked. Drain excess fat.
Add chopped onions and minced garlic to the skillet. Sauté until the onions are translucent.
Stir in frozen peas and diced carrots. Cook for an additional 3-4 minutes until vegetables are slightly tender.
Add condensed cream of mushroom soup and beef broth to the skillet. Season with salt and pepper to taste. Mix well and let it simmer for a few minutes until the mixture thickens slightly.
Layer half of the thinly sliced potatoes in the bottom of the greased baking dish.
Spread half of the beef and vegetable mixture over the potatoes.
Repeat the layers with the remaining potatoes and beef mixture.
Top the casserole with shredded cheddar cheese.
Cover the baking dish with foil and bake in the preheated oven for 40-45 minutes, or until the potatoes are tender.
Remove the foil and bake for an additional 10-15 minutes or until the cheese is melted and bubbly.
Garnish with chopped fresh parsley before serving.

Allow the casserole to cool for a few minutes before serving. This Classic Beef and Potato Casserole is a hearty and comforting dish that's perfect for family dinners. Enjoy!

Chicken Alfredo Bake

Ingredients:

- 8 ounces penne pasta
- 2 cups cooked chicken breast, shredded or diced
- 2 tablespoons butter
- 3 cloves garlic, minced
- 2 cups heavy cream
- 1 cup grated Parmesan cheese
- 1 cup mozzarella cheese, shredded
- Salt and pepper to taste
- 1 teaspoon dried Italian seasoning (optional)
- 1 cup frozen spinach, thawed and drained (optional)
- 1/2 cup sun-dried tomatoes, chopped (optional)
- Fresh parsley, chopped (for garnish)

Instructions:

Preheat your oven to 375°F (190°C). Grease a 9x13-inch baking dish.
Cook the penne pasta according to the package instructions. Drain and set aside.
In a large skillet, melt the butter over medium heat. Add minced garlic and sauté until fragrant, about 1-2 minutes.
Pour in the heavy cream, and bring it to a simmer. Reduce the heat to low.
Stir in the grated Parmesan cheese and continue stirring until the cheese is melted and the sauce is smooth.
Add salt, pepper, and dried Italian seasoning (if using). Adjust seasoning to taste.
Add the cooked chicken to the Alfredo sauce and stir until well coated.
In the prepared baking dish, combine the cooked penne pasta with the chicken Alfredo mixture. If desired, mix in thawed and drained frozen spinach and chopped sun-dried tomatoes.
Sprinkle shredded mozzarella cheese evenly over the top.
Bake in the preheated oven for 20-25 minutes or until the cheese is melted and bubbly, and the edges are golden brown.
Remove from the oven and let it cool for a few minutes.
Garnish with chopped fresh parsley before serving.

This Chicken Alfredo Bake is a creamy and comforting dish with the perfect combination of flavors. Serve it with a side salad or some garlic bread for a complete meal. Enjoy!

Vegetarian Lasagna Casserole

Ingredients:

- 9 lasagna noodles, cooked according to package instructions
- 1 tablespoon olive oil
- 1 onion, finely chopped
- 2 cloves garlic, minced
- 1 bell pepper, diced
- 1 zucchini, diced
- 1 cup mushrooms, sliced
- 1 can (14 ounces) crushed tomatoes
- 1 can (6 ounces) tomato paste
- 1 teaspoon dried oregano
- 1 teaspoon dried basil
- Salt and pepper to taste
- 2 cups ricotta cheese
- 1 egg, beaten
- 3 cups shredded mozzarella cheese
- 1/2 cup grated Parmesan cheese
- Fresh basil or parsley, chopped (for garnish)

Instructions:

Preheat your oven to 375°F (190°C). Grease a 9x13-inch baking dish.
In a large skillet, heat olive oil over medium heat. Add chopped onions and sauté until translucent.
Add minced garlic, bell pepper, zucchini, and mushrooms to the skillet. Sauté until the vegetables are tender.
Stir in crushed tomatoes, tomato paste, dried oregano, dried basil, salt, and pepper. Simmer for about 10-15 minutes to allow the flavors to meld.
In a bowl, mix ricotta cheese with the beaten egg.
Spread a thin layer of the vegetable-tomato sauce on the bottom of the greased baking dish.
Place three cooked lasagna noodles on top of the sauce.
Spread half of the ricotta mixture over the noodles, followed by a layer of the vegetable-tomato sauce. Sprinkle with mozzarella cheese.
Repeat the layers, finishing with a layer of sauce on top. Sprinkle with remaining mozzarella and Parmesan cheese.

Cover the baking dish with foil and bake in the preheated oven for 25 minutes. Remove the foil and bake for an additional 15-20 minutes or until the cheese is melted and bubbly, and the edges are golden brown.
Allow the lasagna casserole to cool for a few minutes before slicing.
Garnish with chopped fresh basil or parsley before serving.

This Vegetarian Lasagna Casserole is a flavorful and hearty dish that's sure to satisfy both vegetarians and non-vegetarians alike. Enjoy!

Tuna Noodle Casserole

Ingredients:

- 8 ounces egg noodles, cooked according to package instructions
- 2 cans (10.5 ounces each) cream of mushroom soup
- 1 cup milk
- 1 cup frozen peas
- 2 cans (5 ounces each) tuna, drained
- 1 cup shredded cheddar cheese
- 1 cup breadcrumbs
- 2 tablespoons butter, melted
- Salt and pepper to taste
- Optional: 1 cup sliced mushrooms, sautéed

Instructions:

Preheat your oven to 375°F (190°C). Grease a 9x13-inch baking dish.
In a large bowl, mix together cream of mushroom soup and milk until well combined.
Add the cooked egg noodles, frozen peas, drained tuna, shredded cheddar cheese, and optional sautéed mushrooms. Mix everything together until well coated with the soup mixture. Season with salt and pepper to taste.
Transfer the mixture to the prepared baking dish, spreading it evenly.
In a small bowl, combine breadcrumbs with melted butter. Sprinkle this mixture evenly over the top of the casserole.
Bake in the preheated oven for 25-30 minutes or until the top is golden brown and the casserole is bubbly.
Remove from the oven and let it cool for a few minutes before serving.
Serve the Tuna Noodle Casserole warm and enjoy!

This Tuna Noodle Casserole is a comforting and classic dish that's quick to prepare.

Feel free to customize it with your favorite ingredients or add a dash of hot sauce or Dijon mustard for extra flavor.

Broccoli and Cheese Chicken Casserole

Ingredients:

- 2 cups cooked chicken breast, shredded or diced
- 4 cups broccoli florets, blanched
- 1 cup mayonnaise
- 1 cup sour cream
- 1 cup shredded cheddar cheese
- 1 cup shredded mozzarella cheese
- 1/2 cup grated Parmesan cheese
- 2 cloves garlic, minced
- 1 teaspoon onion powder
- Salt and pepper to taste
- 1 cup crushed buttery crackers (such as Ritz)
- 2 tablespoons butter, melted
- Fresh parsley, chopped (for garnish)

Instructions:

Preheat your oven to 350°F (175°C). Grease a 9x13-inch baking dish.
In a large bowl, combine the mayonnaise, sour cream, cheddar cheese, mozzarella cheese, Parmesan cheese, minced garlic, onion powder, salt, and pepper. Mix until well combined.
Add the cooked chicken and blanched broccoli to the cheese mixture. Stir until the chicken and broccoli are evenly coated.
Transfer the mixture to the prepared baking dish, spreading it evenly.
In a small bowl, combine the crushed crackers with melted butter. Sprinkle this mixture evenly over the top of the casserole.
Bake in the preheated oven for 25-30 minutes or until the casserole is hot and bubbly, and the top is golden brown.
Remove from the oven and let it cool for a few minutes before serving.
Garnish with chopped fresh parsley before serving.

This Broccoli and Cheese Chicken Casserole is a comforting and satisfying dish that's perfect for a family dinner. The combination of tender chicken, broccoli, and cheesy goodness makes it a crowd-pleaser. Enjoy!

Mexican Taco Casserole

Ingredients:

- 1 pound ground beef
- 1 onion, diced
- 2 cloves garlic, minced
- 1 packet taco seasoning mix
- 1 can (15 ounces) black beans, drained and rinsed
- 1 cup corn kernels (fresh, frozen, or canned)
- 1 cup salsa
- 1 can (4 ounces) diced green chilies
- 1 cup shredded cheddar cheese
- 1 cup shredded Monterey Jack cheese
- 1 cup crushed tortilla chips
- 1 cup sour cream
- 1/2 cup sliced green onions (for garnish)
- Fresh cilantro, chopped (for garnish)

Instructions:

Preheat your oven to 375°F (190°C). Grease a 9x13-inch baking dish.
In a large skillet over medium heat, cook the ground beef until browned. Drain excess fat.
Add diced onions and minced garlic to the skillet. Cook until the onions are softened.
Stir in the taco seasoning mix, black beans, corn, salsa, and diced green chilies.
Simmer for a few minutes until the mixture is heated through.
In the prepared baking dish, layer half of the meat mixture.
Sprinkle half of the shredded cheddar and Monterey Jack cheese over the meat layer.
Spread the remaining meat mixture over the cheese layer.
Top with the remaining shredded cheeses.
Sprinkle the crushed tortilla chips evenly over the top.
Bake in the preheated oven for 20-25 minutes, or until the cheese is melted and bubbly.
Remove from the oven and let it cool for a few minutes.

Drizzle sour cream over the casserole and garnish with sliced green onions and chopped cilantro.

Serve this Mexican Taco Casserole warm, and feel free to customize it with your favorite taco toppings like diced tomatoes, sliced olives, or jalapeños. Enjoy the bold flavors of this delicious casserole!

Eggplant Parmesan Bake

Ingredients:

- 2 large eggplants, thinly sliced
- Salt, for drawing out moisture
- 2 cups marinara sauce
- 1 cup breadcrumbs
- 1 cup grated Parmesan cheese
- 2 cups shredded mozzarella cheese
- 2 large eggs, beaten
- 1 cup all-purpose flour
- Olive oil, for frying
- Fresh basil, chopped (for garnish)
- Salt and pepper to taste

Instructions:

Preheat your oven to 375°F (190°C).
Place the thinly sliced eggplants on a baking sheet and sprinkle each slice with salt. Let them sit for about 30 minutes to draw out excess moisture. Afterward, pat the eggplant slices dry with paper towels.
In three separate shallow bowls, set up a breading station. Place flour in one bowl, beaten eggs in another, and a mixture of breadcrumbs and grated Parmesan cheese in the third bowl.
Dip each eggplant slice into the flour, shaking off excess. Then dip into the beaten eggs, followed by the breadcrumb-Parmesan mixture, pressing the breadcrumbs onto the eggplant to adhere.
In a large skillet, heat olive oil over medium-high heat. Fry the breaded eggplant slices until golden brown on both sides. Place them on paper towels to drain excess oil.
In a greased 9x13-inch baking dish, spread a thin layer of marinara sauce.
Arrange a layer of fried eggplant slices over the marinara sauce.
Sprinkle a portion of shredded mozzarella over the eggplant layer.
Repeat the layers until all the eggplant slices are used, finishing with a layer of marinara sauce and a generous sprinkle of mozzarella on top.
Bake in the preheated oven for 25-30 minutes, or until the cheese is melted and bubbly, and the edges are golden brown.

Remove from the oven and let it cool for a few minutes.
Garnish with chopped fresh basil and season with salt and pepper to taste before serving.

This Eggplant Parmesan Bake is a delicious and satisfying dish. Serve it over pasta or with a side of garlic bread for a complete meal. Enjoy!

Shepherd's Pie

Ingredients:

For the Filling:

- 1 tablespoon olive oil
- 1 onion, finely chopped
- 2 carrots, peeled and diced
- 2 cloves garlic, minced
- 1.5 pounds ground lamb or beef
- 2 tablespoons all-purpose flour
- 1 cup beef or vegetable broth
- 1 tablespoon tomato paste
- 1 teaspoon Worcestershire sauce
- 1 cup frozen peas
- Salt and pepper to taste
- 2 tablespoons chopped fresh thyme or rosemary (or 1 teaspoon dried)

For the Mashed Potato Topping:

- 4 large potatoes, peeled and diced
- 1/2 cup milk
- 4 tablespoons unsalted butter
- Salt and pepper to taste
- 1 cup shredded cheddar cheese (optional)

Instructions:

Preheat your oven to 400°F (200°C).
For the Filling: In a large skillet, heat olive oil over medium heat. Add chopped onions and diced carrots, sauté until softened.
Add minced garlic and ground lamb or beef to the skillet. Cook until the meat is browned.
Sprinkle flour over the meat and vegetables, stir well to combine.
Pour in the broth, add tomato paste, Worcestershire sauce, and herbs. Bring to a simmer and cook until the mixture thickens.
Stir in frozen peas and season with salt and pepper to taste. Remove from heat.

For the Mashed Potato Topping: Boil the peeled and diced potatoes until tender. Drain and mash with milk, butter, salt, and pepper until smooth.

In a greased baking dish, spread the meat and vegetable mixture evenly.

Spoon the mashed potatoes over the top and use a fork to create a decorative pattern.

Optionally, sprinkle shredded cheddar cheese on top of the mashed potatoes.

Bake in the preheated oven for 20-25 minutes or until the top is golden brown.

Remove from the oven and let it cool for a few minutes before serving.

Shepherd's Pie is a comforting and hearty dish that's perfect for a family dinner. Enjoy the layers of flavorful meat and vegetables topped with creamy mashed potatoes!

Spinach and Artichoke Chicken Casserole

Ingredients:

- 4 boneless, skinless chicken breasts
- Salt and pepper to taste
- 1 tablespoon olive oil
- 1 onion, finely chopped
- 3 cloves garlic, minced
- 1 can (14 ounces) artichoke hearts, drained and chopped
- 1 package (10 ounces) frozen chopped spinach, thawed and drained
- 1 cup mayonnaise
- 1 cup sour cream
- 1 cup shredded mozzarella cheese
- 1/2 cup grated Parmesan cheese
- 1 teaspoon garlic powder
- 1 teaspoon onion powder
- 1/2 teaspoon red pepper flakes (optional)
- 1 cup shredded Italian blend cheese (mozzarella, Parmesan, provolone, etc.)
- Fresh parsley, chopped (for garnish)

Instructions:

Preheat your oven to 375°F (190°C). Grease a 9x13-inch baking dish.
Season the chicken breasts with salt and pepper. In a large skillet, heat olive oil over medium-high heat. Brown the chicken on both sides until cooked through. Remove from the skillet and let it rest for a few minutes before shredding or chopping into bite-sized pieces.
In the same skillet, add chopped onions and minced garlic. Sauté until the onions are translucent.
Add chopped artichoke hearts and thawed, drained spinach to the skillet. Cook for an additional 2-3 minutes.
In a large bowl, mix together mayonnaise, sour cream, shredded mozzarella, grated Parmesan, garlic powder, onion powder, and red pepper flakes (if using). Add the cooked chicken and sautéed vegetables to the bowl, stirring until well combined.
Transfer the mixture to the prepared baking dish, spreading it evenly.
Sprinkle the Italian blend cheese over the top.

Bake in the preheated oven for 25-30 minutes or until the casserole is hot and bubbly, and the cheese is melted and golden.
Remove from the oven and let it cool for a few minutes.
Garnish with chopped fresh parsley before serving.

This Spinach and Artichoke Chicken Casserole is a creamy and flavorful dish that combines the classic flavors of spinach and artichoke dip with tender chicken. Serve it over rice, pasta, or with a side of crusty bread. Enjoy!

Sausage and Mushroom Breakfast Casserole

Ingredients:

- 1 pound breakfast sausage (pork or turkey), crumbled
- 1 tablespoon olive oil
- 1 onion, finely chopped
- 8 ounces mushrooms, sliced
- 1 red bell pepper, diced
- 6 large eggs
- 1 1/2 cups milk
- 1 teaspoon Dijon mustard
- Salt and pepper to taste
- 4 cups cubed bread (such as French or Italian bread)
- 1 1/2 cups shredded cheddar cheese
- 1/2 cup grated Parmesan cheese
- Fresh parsley, chopped (for garnish)

Instructions:

Preheat your oven to 350°F (175°C). Grease a 9x13-inch baking dish.
In a large skillet over medium heat, cook the crumbled sausage until browned. Remove excess fat if necessary.
In the same skillet, add olive oil, chopped onion, sliced mushrooms, and diced red bell pepper. Sauté until the vegetables are softened.
In a large mixing bowl, whisk together eggs, milk, Dijon mustard, salt, and pepper.
Add the cubed bread to the egg mixture, ensuring that all the bread is coated.
Stir in the cooked sausage and sautéed vegetables.
Fold in shredded cheddar cheese and grated Parmesan cheese.
Transfer the mixture to the prepared baking dish, spreading it evenly.
Let the casserole sit for about 15 minutes to allow the bread to absorb the liquid.
Bake in the preheated oven for 40-45 minutes or until the casserole is set, and the top is golden brown.
Remove from the oven and let it cool for a few minutes.
Garnish with chopped fresh parsley before serving.

This Sausage and Mushroom Breakfast Casserole is a hearty and flavorful way to start your day. It's perfect for brunch or when you have guests over. Enjoy!

Sweet Potato and Black Bean Enchilada Casserole

Ingredients:

- 2 large sweet potatoes, peeled and diced
- 1 tablespoon olive oil
- 1 onion, finely chopped
- 2 cloves garlic, minced
- 1 can (15 ounces) black beans, drained and rinsed
- 1 can (15 ounces) corn kernels, drained
- 1 can (10 ounces) enchilada sauce
- 1 teaspoon ground cumin
- 1 teaspoon chili powder
- Salt and pepper to taste
- 8-10 corn tortillas
- 2 cups shredded Mexican blend cheese
- Fresh cilantro, chopped (for garnish)
- Sour cream (optional, for serving)

Instructions:

Preheat your oven to 375°F (190°C). Grease a 9x13-inch baking dish.

In a large pot of boiling water, cook the diced sweet potatoes until just tender. Drain and set aside.

In a large skillet, heat olive oil over medium heat. Add chopped onions and sauté until translucent.

Add minced garlic, black beans, and corn to the skillet. Cook for an additional 2-3 minutes.

Stir in the cooked sweet potatoes, enchilada sauce, ground cumin, chili powder, salt, and pepper. Mix well and let it simmer for a few minutes.

In the prepared baking dish, spread a thin layer of the sweet potato and black bean mixture.

Layer corn tortillas on top of the mixture, followed by more sweet potato and black bean mixture. Repeat until you've used all the filling, finishing with a layer of tortillas on top.

Sprinkle shredded Mexican blend cheese over the top.

Bake in the preheated oven for 20-25 minutes or until the cheese is melted and bubbly, and the edges are golden brown.

Remove from the oven and let it cool for a few minutes.
Garnish with chopped fresh cilantro before serving.
Serve with a dollop of sour cream if desired.

This Sweet Potato and Black Bean Enchilada Casserole is a flavorful and satisfying dish that's perfect for a meatless dinner. Enjoy the combination of sweet potatoes, black beans, and spices in every bite!

Chicken and Rice Casserole

Ingredients:

- 1 1/2 cups long-grain white rice
- 3 cups cooked and shredded chicken (rotisserie chicken works well)
- 1 tablespoon olive oil
- 1 onion, finely chopped
- 2 cloves garlic, minced
- 1 cup carrots, diced
- 1 cup frozen peas
- 1 cup frozen corn kernels
- 1 can (10.5 ounces) condensed cream of mushroom soup
- 2 cups chicken broth
- 1 teaspoon dried thyme
- Salt and pepper to taste
- 1 cup shredded cheddar cheese
- Fresh parsley, chopped (for garnish)

Instructions:

Preheat your oven to 350°F (175°C). Grease a 9x13-inch baking dish.
Cook the white rice according to package instructions.
In a large skillet, heat olive oil over medium heat. Add chopped onions and sauté until translucent.
Add minced garlic, diced carrots, frozen peas, and frozen corn to the skillet.
Sauté until the vegetables are slightly tender.
In a large mixing bowl, combine the cooked and shredded chicken with the sautéed vegetables.
In a separate bowl, whisk together condensed cream of mushroom soup, chicken broth, dried thyme, salt, and pepper.
Add the cooked rice to the chicken and vegetable mixture, followed by the soup mixture. Mix everything until well combined.
Transfer the mixture to the prepared baking dish, spreading it evenly.
Sprinkle shredded cheddar cheese over the top.
Bake in the preheated oven for 25-30 minutes or until the casserole is hot and bubbly, and the cheese is melted and golden.
Remove from the oven and let it cool for a few minutes.

Garnish with chopped fresh parsley before serving.

This Chicken and Rice Casserole is a comforting and easy-to-make dish that's perfect for a family dinner. Enjoy the hearty combination of chicken, vegetables, rice, and creamy sauce!

Zucchini and Tomato Gratin

Ingredients:

- 2-3 large zucchini, thinly sliced
- 4-5 medium-sized tomatoes, thinly sliced
- 2 tablespoons olive oil
- 2 cloves garlic, minced
- 1 teaspoon dried thyme
- Salt and pepper to taste
- 1 cup grated Parmesan cheese
- 1 cup shredded mozzarella cheese
- 1/2 cup breadcrumbs
- Fresh basil, chopped (for garnish)

Instructions:

Preheat your oven to 375°F (190°C). Grease a baking dish (such as a 9x13-inch dish) with olive oil or cooking spray.
In a large skillet, heat olive oil over medium heat. Add minced garlic and sauté for about 1 minute until fragrant.
Add the thinly sliced zucchini to the skillet. Season with dried thyme, salt, and pepper. Cook for 3-4 minutes, stirring occasionally, until the zucchini is slightly tender. Remove from heat.
In the prepared baking dish, arrange a layer of the sautéed zucchini.
Place a layer of thinly sliced tomatoes over the zucchini.
Sprinkle a portion of grated Parmesan and shredded mozzarella over the tomato layer.
Repeat the layers until you've used all the zucchini and tomatoes, finishing with a layer of cheese on top.
In a small bowl, mix breadcrumbs with a bit of olive oil to moisten. Sprinkle this breadcrumb mixture evenly over the top.
Bake in the preheated oven for 25-30 minutes or until the vegetables are tender, and the top is golden brown and bubbly.
Remove from the oven and let it cool for a few minutes.
Garnish with chopped fresh basil before serving.

This Zucchini and Tomato Gratin is a flavorful and colorful dish that makes a wonderful side or even a light vegetarian main course. Enjoy the combination of zucchini, tomatoes, and melted cheese!

Buffalo Chicken Mac and Cheese Bake

Ingredients:

- 8 ounces elbow macaroni or your preferred pasta
- 2 cups cooked and shredded chicken (rotisserie chicken works well)
- 1/2 cup unsalted butter
- 1/2 cup all-purpose flour
- 3 cups whole milk
- 2 cups shredded sharp cheddar cheese
- 1 cup shredded mozzarella cheese
- 1/2 cup buffalo sauce (adjust to taste)
- 1/2 cup blue cheese dressing
- Salt and pepper to taste
- 1 cup panko breadcrumbs
- 2 tablespoons melted butter
- Green onions, chopped (for garnish)

Instructions:

Preheat your oven to 375°F (190°C). Grease a 9x13-inch baking dish.
Cook the elbow macaroni according to package instructions. Drain and set aside.
In a large pot, melt 1/2 cup of butter over medium heat. Stir in the flour to create a roux, cooking for 1-2 minutes until it turns golden brown.
Gradually whisk in the whole milk, stirring continuously to avoid lumps. Continue cooking until the mixture thickens.
Reduce the heat to low, and add the shredded cheddar and mozzarella cheese. Stir until the cheese is melted and the sauce is smooth.
Stir in the buffalo sauce and blue cheese dressing. Season with salt and pepper to taste.
Add the cooked and shredded chicken to the cheese sauce, mixing until well combined.
In the prepared baking dish, combine the cooked pasta with the buffalo chicken and cheese sauce, ensuring everything is evenly coated.
In a small bowl, mix panko breadcrumbs with melted butter. Sprinkle this mixture evenly over the top.
Bake in the preheated oven for 20-25 minutes or until the top is golden brown and the casserole is bubbly.

Remove from the oven and let it cool for a few minutes.
Garnish with chopped green onions before serving.

This Buffalo Chicken Mac and Cheese Bake is a spicy and cheesy twist on the classic comfort food. Enjoy the bold flavors of buffalo sauce and blue cheese in every bite!

Mediterranean Quinoa Casserole

Ingredients:

- 1 cup quinoa, rinsed and drained
- 2 cups vegetable broth or water
- 2 tablespoons olive oil
- 1 onion, finely chopped
- 3 cloves garlic, minced
- 1 red bell pepper, diced
- 1 yellow bell pepper, diced
- 1 zucchini, diced
- 1 cup cherry tomatoes, halved
- 1 cup kalamata olives, pitted and halved
- 1/2 cup crumbled feta cheese
- 1 teaspoon dried oregano
- 1 teaspoon dried basil
- Salt and pepper to taste
- Juice of 1 lemon
- Fresh parsley, chopped (for garnish)

Instructions:

Preheat your oven to 375°F (190°C). Grease a 9x13-inch baking dish.
In a medium saucepan, combine quinoa and vegetable broth (or water). Bring to a boil, then reduce heat to low, cover, and simmer for about 15 minutes or until quinoa is cooked and liquid is absorbed. Fluff the quinoa with a fork.
In a large skillet, heat olive oil over medium heat. Add chopped onions and sauté until translucent.
Add minced garlic, diced red and yellow bell peppers, and diced zucchini to the skillet. Sauté until the vegetables are slightly tender.
Stir in halved cherry tomatoes and kalamata olives. Cook for an additional 2-3 minutes.
In a large mixing bowl, combine the cooked quinoa with the sautéed vegetables. Add crumbled feta cheese, dried oregano, dried basil, salt, and pepper. Mix well.
Transfer the mixture to the prepared baking dish, spreading it evenly.
Drizzle the lemon juice over the top.
Bake in the preheated oven for 20-25 minutes or until the casserole is heated through, and the edges are golden brown.

Remove from the oven and let it cool for a few minutes.
Garnish with chopped fresh parsley before serving.

This Mediterranean Quinoa Casserole is a healthy and flavorful dish inspired by the vibrant flavors of the Mediterranean cuisine. Enjoy the combination of quinoa, colorful vegetables, olives, and feta cheese!

Turkey Tetrazzini

Ingredients:

- 8 ounces spaghetti or fettuccine, cooked according to package instructions
- 1/2 cup unsalted butter
- 1/2 cup all-purpose flour
- 4 cups turkey or chicken broth
- 2 cups milk
- 1/2 cup dry white wine (optional)
- 1 teaspoon salt
- 1/2 teaspoon black pepper
- 1/2 teaspoon garlic powder
- 2 cups cooked turkey, shredded or diced
- 1 cup frozen peas
- 1 cup sliced mushrooms
- 1 cup grated Parmesan cheese
- 1 cup shredded mozzarella cheese
- 1/2 cup breadcrumbs
- Chopped fresh parsley (for garnish)

Instructions:

Preheat your oven to 375°F (190°C). Grease a 9x13-inch baking dish.
In a large pot, melt the butter over medium heat. Add the flour and whisk continuously to create a roux. Cook for 2-3 minutes until it's lightly golden.
Gradually whisk in the turkey or chicken broth, followed by the milk and white wine (if using). Continue whisking to avoid lumps.
Season the sauce with salt, black pepper, and garlic powder. Simmer until it thickens, stirring occasionally.
Add the cooked and shredded turkey, frozen peas, sliced mushrooms, and Parmesan cheese to the sauce. Stir until well combined.
In the prepared baking dish, mix the cooked pasta with the turkey and sauce mixture, ensuring everything is evenly coated.
Sprinkle shredded mozzarella cheese over the top.
In a small bowl, mix breadcrumbs with a bit of melted butter. Sprinkle this breadcrumb mixture evenly over the casserole.
Bake in the preheated oven for 25-30 minutes or until the top is golden brown and the casserole is bubbly.

Remove from the oven and let it cool for a few minutes.
Garnish with chopped fresh parsley before serving.

This Turkey Tetrazzini is a comforting and hearty dish, perfect for using leftover turkey from Thanksgiving or any other occasion. Enjoy the creamy and cheesy goodness of this classic casserole!

Ratatouille Bake

Ingredients:

- 1 large eggplant, thinly sliced
- 2 medium zucchini, thinly sliced
- 2 medium yellow squash, thinly sliced
- 3 large tomatoes, thinly sliced
- 1 large red onion, thinly sliced
- 3 cloves garlic, minced
- 1/4 cup olive oil
- 1 teaspoon dried thyme
- 1 teaspoon dried rosemary
- Salt and pepper to taste
- 1 can (14 ounces) crushed tomatoes
- 1/2 cup grated Parmesan cheese
- 1 cup shredded mozzarella cheese
- Fresh basil or parsley, chopped (for garnish)

Instructions:

Preheat your oven to 375°F (190°C). Grease a 9x13-inch baking dish.
In a large bowl, toss the thinly sliced eggplant, zucchini, yellow squash, tomatoes, and red onion with minced garlic, olive oil, dried thyme, dried rosemary, salt, and pepper.
Arrange the vegetable slices in the prepared baking dish, alternating and overlapping them in rows.
Pour the crushed tomatoes over the top, spreading it evenly.
Sprinkle grated Parmesan cheese over the vegetables.
Cover the baking dish with aluminum foil and bake in the preheated oven for 45-50 minutes, or until the vegetables are tender.
Remove the foil and sprinkle shredded mozzarella cheese over the top.
Bake for an additional 10-15 minutes or until the cheese is melted and bubbly, and the edges are golden brown.
Remove from the oven and let it cool for a few minutes.
Garnish with chopped fresh basil or parsley before serving.

This Ratatouille Bake is a colorful and flavorful dish that showcases the beauty of seasonal vegetables. It's a great side dish or can be served on its own with crusty bread or as a topping for pasta or rice. Enjoy the rich combination of flavors!

BBQ Pulled Pork Mac and Cheese

Ingredients:

For the Pulled Pork:

- 2 pounds pork shoulder or pork butt
- Salt and pepper to taste
- 1 cup barbecue sauce (store-bought or homemade)
- 1 cup chicken broth

For the Mac and Cheese:

- 8 ounces elbow macaroni or your favorite pasta
- 4 tablespoons unsalted butter
- 1/4 cup all-purpose flour
- 2 cups whole milk
- 2 cups shredded sharp cheddar cheese
- 1 cup shredded mozzarella cheese
- 1/2 teaspoon garlic powder
- Salt and pepper to taste
- 1 cup barbecue pulled pork (from the prepared pulled pork)
- 1/4 cup barbecue sauce (for mixing with pulled pork)
- Green onions, chopped (for garnish)

Instructions:

For the Pulled Pork:

    Preheat your oven to 325°F (163°C).
    Season the pork shoulder with salt and pepper. Place it in a roasting pan.
    In a bowl, mix together barbecue sauce and chicken broth. Pour the mixture over the pork.
    Cover the roasting pan with foil and roast in the preheated oven for 3-4 hours or until the pork is tender and easily shredded with a fork.
    Shred the pork and mix it with additional barbecue sauce, set aside.

For the Mac and Cheese:

    Cook the elbow macaroni according to package instructions. Drain and set aside.

In a large pot, melt butter over medium heat. Stir in the flour to create a roux. Cook for 1-2 minutes until it's lightly golden.

Gradually whisk in the whole milk, stirring continuously to avoid lumps. Continue whisking until the mixture thickens.

Reduce the heat to low, and add shredded cheddar and mozzarella cheese. Stir until the cheese is melted and the sauce is smooth.

Season the sauce with garlic powder, salt, and pepper.

Add the cooked macaroni to the cheese sauce, mixing until well combined.

Stir in the barbecue pulled pork and additional barbecue sauce, ensuring everything is evenly coated.

Serve the BBQ Pulled Pork Mac and Cheese warm, garnished with chopped green onions.

This dish combines the comfort of mac and cheese with the savory goodness of BBQ pulled pork, creating a flavorful and hearty meal. Enjoy!

Creamy Mushroom and Wild Rice Casserole

Ingredients:

- 1 cup wild rice, uncooked
- 4 cups vegetable or chicken broth
- 3 tablespoons butter
- 1 onion, finely chopped
- 3 cloves garlic, minced
- 1 pound mushrooms, sliced (a mix of different varieties adds depth of flavor)
- 1/4 cup all-purpose flour
- 2 cups milk (whole or 2%)
- 1 cup sour cream
- 1 teaspoon dried thyme
- Salt and pepper to taste
- 1/2 cup grated Parmesan cheese
- 1 cup shredded Gruyère or Swiss cheese
- Fresh parsley, chopped (for garnish)

Instructions:

Preheat your oven to 350°F (175°C). Grease a 9x13-inch baking dish.
In a medium saucepan, combine the wild rice and broth. Bring to a boil, then reduce heat to low, cover, and simmer for about 45-55 minutes, or until the rice is tender and has absorbed the liquid. Fluff the rice with a fork.
In a large skillet, melt butter over medium heat. Add chopped onions and sauté until translucent.
Add minced garlic and sliced mushrooms to the skillet. Cook until the mushrooms release their moisture and become golden brown.
Sprinkle flour over the mushroom mixture and stir to combine. Cook for an additional 2-3 minutes.
Gradually whisk in the milk, stirring constantly to avoid lumps. Continue cooking until the mixture thickens.
Stir in sour cream, dried thyme, salt, and pepper.
In a large mixing bowl, combine the cooked wild rice with the mushroom and cream mixture.
Fold in grated Parmesan cheese and shredded Gruyère or Swiss cheese until well combined.

Transfer the mixture to the prepared baking dish, spreading it evenly.
Bake in the preheated oven for 25-30 minutes or until the casserole is hot and bubbly, and the top is golden brown.
Remove from the oven and let it cool for a few minutes.
Garnish with chopped fresh parsley before serving.

This Creamy Mushroom and Wild Rice Casserole is a rich and comforting dish with a delightful combination of flavors and textures. Enjoy the earthiness of mushrooms and the nuttiness of wild rice in every bite!

Shrimp and Grits Casserole

Ingredients:

For the Grits:

- 1 cup stone-ground grits
- 4 cups water
- 1 cup milk
- 2 tablespoons butter
- Salt to taste
- 1 cup shredded sharp cheddar cheese

For the Shrimp:

- 1 pound large shrimp, peeled and deveined
- 1 tablespoon olive oil
- 1 onion, finely chopped
- 1 bell pepper, diced
- 3 cloves garlic, minced
- 1 cup diced tomatoes
- 1/2 cup chicken broth
- 1 teaspoon Cajun seasoning (adjust to taste)
- Salt and pepper to taste
- 1/4 cup chopped green onions (for garnish)
- Lemon wedges (for serving)

Instructions:

For the Grits:

> In a medium saucepan, bring water and milk to a boil.
> Gradually whisk in the grits, reduce heat to low, and simmer, stirring frequently, until the grits are thick and creamy.
> Stir in butter, salt, and shredded cheddar cheese until well combined. Remove from heat and set aside.

For the Shrimp:

> Preheat your oven to 375°F (190°C). Grease a 9x13-inch baking dish.

In a large skillet, heat olive oil over medium-high heat. Add chopped onions and diced bell pepper, sauté until softened.

Add minced garlic and cook for an additional 1-2 minutes.

Stir in diced tomatoes, chicken broth, Cajun seasoning, salt, and pepper. Simmer for about 5 minutes.

Add the peeled and deveined shrimp to the skillet, cooking until they turn pink and opaque.

Spread the cooked grits evenly in the prepared baking dish.

Spoon the shrimp and vegetable mixture over the grits layer.

Bake in the preheated oven for 20-25 minutes or until the casserole is hot and bubbly.

Remove from the oven and let it cool for a few minutes.

Garnish with chopped green onions and serve with lemon wedges on the side.

This Shrimp and Grits Casserole is a Southern-inspired dish that combines the rich and creamy texture of grits with flavorful Cajun-spiced shrimp. It's a comforting and satisfying meal that's perfect for any occasion!

Italian Sausage and Peppers Bake

Ingredients:

- 1 pound Italian sausage links (sweet or hot), cut into bite-sized pieces
- 2 tablespoons olive oil
- 1 large onion, thinly sliced
- 2 bell peppers (any color), thinly sliced
- 1 yellow or red onion, thinly sliced
- 3 cloves garlic, minced
- 1 can (14 ounces) crushed tomatoes
- 1 teaspoon dried oregano
- 1 teaspoon dried basil
- Salt and pepper to taste
- 1/2 teaspoon red pepper flakes (optional)
- 1 cup shredded mozzarella cheese
- Fresh basil or parsley, chopped (for garnish)

Instructions:

Preheat your oven to 375°F (190°C). Grease a 9x13-inch baking dish.
In a large skillet, heat olive oil over medium-high heat. Add Italian sausage pieces and brown on all sides. Remove the sausage from the skillet and set aside.
In the same skillet, add sliced onions and bell peppers. Sauté until the vegetables are softened.
Add minced garlic to the skillet and cook for an additional 1-2 minutes until fragrant.
Stir in crushed tomatoes, dried oregano, dried basil, salt, pepper, and red pepper flakes (if using). Simmer for about 5 minutes.
Place the browned Italian sausage back into the skillet, mixing it with the tomato and pepper mixture.
Transfer the sausage and peppers mixture to the prepared baking dish, spreading it evenly.
Sprinkle shredded mozzarella cheese over the top.
Bake in the preheated oven for 25-30 minutes or until the cheese is melted and bubbly, and the edges are golden brown.
Remove from the oven and let it cool for a few minutes.
Garnish with chopped fresh basil or parsley before serving.

This Italian Sausage and Peppers Bake is a flavorful and comforting dish that captures the essence of classic Italian flavors. Serve it over pasta, rice, or with a side of crusty bread. Enjoy!

Caprese Pasta Bake

Ingredients:

- 16 ounces (1 pound) penne or your favorite pasta
- 2 tablespoons olive oil
- 3 cloves garlic, minced
- 1 pint cherry tomatoes, halved
- 1/2 cup sun-dried tomatoes, chopped
- 8 ounces fresh mozzarella cheese, cut into small cubes
- 1/2 cup grated Parmesan cheese
- 1/4 cup fresh basil, chopped
- 1/4 cup fresh parsley, chopped
- Salt and pepper to taste
- Balsamic glaze (for drizzling)

Instructions:

Preheat your oven to 375°F (190°C). Grease a 9x13-inch baking dish.
Cook the pasta according to package instructions until al dente. Drain and set aside.
In a large skillet, heat olive oil over medium heat. Add minced garlic and sauté for 1-2 minutes until fragrant.
Add halved cherry tomatoes and sun-dried tomatoes to the skillet. Cook for an additional 2-3 minutes until the tomatoes are slightly softened.
In a large mixing bowl, combine the cooked pasta with the tomato mixture.
Add fresh mozzarella cubes, grated Parmesan cheese, chopped basil, and chopped parsley. Toss everything together until well combined.
Season with salt and pepper to taste.
Transfer the pasta mixture to the prepared baking dish, spreading it evenly.
Bake in the preheated oven for 20-25 minutes or until the pasta is hot and bubbly, and the cheese is melted and golden brown.
Remove from the oven and let it cool for a few minutes.
Drizzle balsamic glaze over the top before serving.

This Caprese Pasta Bake is a delightful and flavorful dish that combines the classic flavors of Caprese salad with the comfort of baked pasta. Serve it as a main dish or a side for a delicious and satisfying meal!

Green Bean Casserole

Ingredients:

- 1 1/2 pounds fresh green beans, trimmed and cut into bite-sized pieces
- 1 tablespoon olive oil
- 1 medium onion, finely chopped
- 2 cloves garlic, minced
- 8 ounces mushrooms, sliced
- Salt and pepper to taste
- 2 tablespoons all-purpose flour
- 1 cup chicken or vegetable broth
- 1 cup milk
- 1 teaspoon soy sauce
- 1/2 teaspoon Worcestershire sauce
- 2 cans (14 ounces each) French-style green beans, drained
- 1 1/2 cups crispy fried onions

Instructions:

Preheat your oven to 375°F (190°C). Grease a 9x13-inch baking dish.

Bring a large pot of water to a boil. Add the fresh green beans and cook for 3-4 minutes until they are bright green and slightly tender. Drain and transfer the beans to a bowl of ice water to stop the cooking process. Drain again and set aside.

In a large skillet, heat olive oil over medium heat. Add chopped onions and sauté until translucent.

Add minced garlic and sliced mushrooms to the skillet. Cook until the mushrooms release their moisture and become golden brown. Season with salt and pepper.

Sprinkle flour over the mushroom mixture and stir to combine. Cook for 1-2 minutes.

Gradually whisk in the chicken or vegetable broth and milk, stirring constantly to avoid lumps. Continue whisking until the mixture thickens.

Stir in soy sauce and Worcestershire sauce. Simmer for a few minutes until the sauce has thickened.

In a large mixing bowl, combine the blanched fresh green beans, French-style green beans, and the mushroom sauce. Mix well to coat the beans evenly.

Transfer the mixture to the prepared baking dish, spreading it evenly.
Bake in the preheated oven for 25-30 minutes or until the casserole is hot and bubbly.
Remove from the oven and sprinkle crispy fried onions over the top.
Bake for an additional 5 minutes or until the onions are golden brown and crispy.
Remove from the oven and let it cool for a few minutes before serving.

This Green Bean Casserole is a classic side dish that's perfect for holidays or any family gathering. Enjoy the creamy mushroom sauce and crispy fried onions combined with the freshness of green beans!

Lemon Garlic Chicken and Rice Casserole

Ingredients:

- 1 1/2 cups long-grain white rice
- 3 cups chicken broth
- 4 boneless, skinless chicken breasts
- Salt and pepper to taste
- 2 tablespoons olive oil
- 4 cloves garlic, minced
- 1 teaspoon dried thyme
- 1 teaspoon dried rosemary
- Zest of 1 lemon
- Juice of 1 lemon
- 1/2 cup chicken broth (additional)
- 1/2 cup heavy cream
- 1 cup frozen peas
- Fresh parsley, chopped (for garnish)

Instructions:

Preheat your oven to 375°F (190°C). Grease a 9x13-inch baking dish.

In a medium saucepan, bring the chicken broth to a boil. Add the rice, reduce heat to low, cover, and simmer for about 15 minutes or until the rice is partially cooked. Remove from heat and set aside.

Season the chicken breasts with salt and pepper.

In a large oven-safe skillet, heat olive oil over medium-high heat. Add the seasoned chicken breasts and sear on both sides until golden brown. Remove the chicken from the skillet and set aside.

In the same skillet, add minced garlic, dried thyme, dried rosemary, lemon zest, and lemon juice. Cook for 1-2 minutes until fragrant.

Pour in the additional 1/2 cup of chicken broth and heavy cream. Bring the mixture to a simmer.

Add the partially cooked rice to the skillet, mixing it with the garlic and herb mixture.

Place the seared chicken breasts on top of the rice.

Add frozen peas to the skillet, distributing them evenly.

Transfer the skillet to the preheated oven and bake for 25-30 minutes or until the chicken is cooked through, and the rice is tender.
Remove from the oven and let it cool for a few minutes.
Garnish with chopped fresh parsley before serving.

This Lemon Garlic Chicken and Rice Casserole is a bright and flavorful dish that combines the zesty taste of lemon with aromatic garlic and herbs. Enjoy the tender chicken and perfectly cooked rice in this comforting casserole!

Beef and Broccoli Quinoa Bake

Ingredients:

- 1 cup quinoa, rinsed and drained
- 2 cups beef broth
- 1 pound ground beef
- 1 onion, finely chopped
- 2 cloves garlic, minced
- 2 cups broccoli florets, steamed or blanched
- 1 cup shredded cheddar cheese
- 1/4 cup soy sauce
- 2 tablespoons oyster sauce
- 1 tablespoon sesame oil
- 1 teaspoon ground ginger
- Salt and pepper to taste
- Green onions, chopped (for garnish)

Instructions:

Preheat your oven to 375°F (190°C). Grease a 9x13-inch baking dish.
In a medium saucepan, combine quinoa and beef broth. Bring to a boil, then reduce heat to low, cover, and simmer for about 15 minutes or until quinoa is cooked and liquid is absorbed. Fluff the quinoa with a fork.
In a large skillet, cook ground beef over medium heat until browned. Drain excess fat.
Add chopped onions and minced garlic to the skillet. Sauté until the onions are translucent.
Stir in steamed or blanched broccoli florets, cooked quinoa, shredded cheddar cheese, soy sauce, oyster sauce, sesame oil, ground ginger, salt, and pepper. Mix until well combined.
Transfer the mixture to the prepared baking dish, spreading it evenly.
Bake in the preheated oven for 20-25 minutes or until the casserole is hot and bubbly, and the edges are golden brown.
Remove from the oven and let it cool for a few minutes.
Garnish with chopped green onions before serving.

This Beef and Broccoli Quinoa Bake is a wholesome and flavorful dish that combines the richness of beef with the nutritional goodness of quinoa and broccoli. Enjoy the savory and satisfying flavors in every bite!

Chicken Enchilada Casserole

Ingredients:

- 2 cups shredded cooked chicken (rotisserie chicken works well)
- 1 can (15 ounces) black beans, drained and rinsed
- 1 cup corn kernels (fresh, frozen, or canned)
- 1 cup diced bell peppers (a mix of colors)
- 1 cup diced onion
- 1 can (10 ounces) red enchilada sauce
- 1 can (4 ounces) diced green chilies, drained
- 1 teaspoon ground cumin
- 1 teaspoon chili powder
- Salt and pepper to taste
- 2 cups shredded Mexican blend cheese
- 10 small corn tortillas
- Fresh cilantro, chopped (for garnish)
- Sour cream and sliced jalapeños (optional, for serving)

Instructions:

Preheat your oven to 375°F (190°C). Grease a 9x13-inch baking dish.
In a large mixing bowl, combine shredded chicken, black beans, corn, diced bell peppers, and diced onion.
In a separate bowl, mix together the red enchilada sauce, diced green chilies, ground cumin, chili powder, salt, and pepper.
Add half of the enchilada sauce mixture to the chicken and vegetable mixture. Mix until well combined.
Cut the corn tortillas into bite-sized pieces.
Layer half of the tortilla pieces in the bottom of the prepared baking dish.
Spoon half of the chicken and vegetable mixture over the tortillas.
Sprinkle half of the shredded Mexican blend cheese over the chicken mixture.
Repeat the layers with the remaining tortilla pieces, chicken mixture, and cheese.
Pour the remaining enchilada sauce mixture over the top.
Bake in the preheated oven for 25-30 minutes or until the casserole is hot and bubbly, and the cheese is melted and golden brown.
Remove from the oven and let it cool for a few minutes.
Garnish with chopped fresh cilantro.

Serve with optional toppings such as sour cream and sliced jalapeños.

This Chicken Enchilada Casserole is a flavorful and easy-to-make dish that captures the essence of classic enchiladas. Enjoy the delicious combination of chicken, beans, veggies, and gooey melted cheese!

Cajun Jambalaya Casserole

Ingredients:

- 1 pound boneless, skinless chicken thighs, diced
- 1 pound Andouille sausage, sliced
- 1 tablespoon Cajun seasoning
- 1 tablespoon olive oil
- 1 onion, finely chopped
- 1 bell pepper, diced
- 3 celery stalks, diced
- 3 cloves garlic, minced
- 1 can (14 ounces) diced tomatoes, undrained
- 1 cup long-grain white rice
- 2 1/2 cups chicken broth
- 1 teaspoon dried thyme
- 1 teaspoon dried oregano
- 1/2 teaspoon paprika
- Salt and pepper to taste
- 1 pound large shrimp, peeled and deveined
- 1/2 cup green onions, chopped
- Fresh parsley, chopped (for garnish)

Instructions:

Preheat your oven to 375°F (190°C). Grease a large baking dish.
In a bowl, toss the diced chicken with Cajun seasoning until evenly coated.
In a large skillet, heat olive oil over medium-high heat. Add the seasoned chicken and Andouille sausage. Cook until the chicken is browned and the sausage is slightly crisp. Remove from the skillet and set aside.
In the same skillet, add chopped onion, diced bell pepper, diced celery, and minced garlic. Sauté until the vegetables are softened.
Stir in diced tomatoes (with their juice), rice, chicken broth, dried thyme, dried oregano, paprika, salt, and pepper. Bring the mixture to a boil.
Reduce heat to low, cover, and simmer for about 15 minutes or until the rice is partially cooked.
Stir in the browned chicken and sausage mixture, along with the peeled and deveined shrimp.

Transfer the mixture to the prepared baking dish, spreading it evenly.
Cover the baking dish with foil and bake in the preheated oven for 20-25 minutes or until the rice is tender, and the shrimp are cooked through.
Remove from the oven and let it cool for a few minutes.
Garnish with chopped green onions and fresh parsley before serving.

This Cajun Jambalaya Casserole is a flavorful and hearty dish that brings the bold and spicy flavors of traditional jambalaya in a convenient casserole form. Enjoy the Cajun-inspired goodness!

Cheesy Hash Brown Casserole

Ingredients:

- 1 package (30 ounces) frozen shredded hash browns, thawed
- 1/2 cup unsalted butter, melted
- 1 can (10.5 ounces) condensed cream of chicken soup
- 1 cup sour cream
- 1 small onion, finely chopped
- 2 cups shredded cheddar cheese
- 1 teaspoon garlic powder
- 1/2 teaspoon salt
- 1/4 teaspoon black pepper
- 2 cups crispy fried onions (optional, for topping)

Instructions:

Preheat your oven to 350°F (175°C). Grease a 9x13-inch baking dish.
In a large mixing bowl, combine the thawed shredded hash browns and melted butter. Mix well to coat the hash browns.
In another bowl, mix together the condensed cream of chicken soup, sour cream, chopped onion, shredded cheddar cheese, garlic powder, salt, and black pepper.
Add the soup mixture to the hash brown mixture, stirring until everything is well combined.
Transfer the mixture to the prepared baking dish, spreading it evenly.
If desired, sprinkle crispy fried onions over the top for added crunch.
Bake in the preheated oven for 45-50 minutes or until the casserole is hot and bubbly, and the top is golden brown.
Remove from the oven and let it cool for a few minutes before serving.

This Cheesy Hash Brown Casserole is a classic and comforting side dish that's perfect for brunches, potlucks, or family gatherings. Enjoy the creamy and cheesy goodness of this easy-to-make casserole!

Egg and Sausage Breakfast Bake

Ingredients:

- 1 pound breakfast sausage (pork or turkey), crumbled and cooked
- 8 large eggs
- 1 cup milk
- 1 teaspoon Dijon mustard
- 1/2 teaspoon salt
- 1/4 teaspoon black pepper
- 1 cup shredded cheddar cheese
- 1 cup diced bell peppers (any color)
- 1 cup diced onions
- 1 cup diced tomatoes
- 1 tablespoon chopped fresh parsley (for garnish)

Instructions:

Preheat your oven to 350°F (175°C). Grease a 9x13-inch baking dish.
In a skillet, cook and crumble the breakfast sausage over medium heat until browned. Drain any excess fat.
In a large mixing bowl, whisk together the eggs, milk, Dijon mustard, salt, and black pepper.
Stir in the cooked sausage, shredded cheddar cheese, diced bell peppers, onions, and tomatoes.
Pour the mixture into the prepared baking dish, spreading it evenly.
Bake in the preheated oven for 25-30 minutes or until the eggs are set and the top is golden brown.
Remove from the oven and let it cool for a few minutes.
Garnish with chopped fresh parsley before serving.

This Egg and Sausage Breakfast Bake is a satisfying and flavorful way to start your day.

It's perfect for brunch or when you have guests over for breakfast. Enjoy the

combination of savory sausage, eggs, and vegetables in this hearty and delicious dish!

Pesto Chicken and Penne Casserole

Ingredients:

- 12 ounces penne pasta, cooked according to package instructions
- 2 cups cooked and shredded chicken breast
- 1 cup cherry tomatoes, halved
- 1/2 cup sun-dried tomatoes, chopped
- 1/2 cup pesto sauce (store-bought or homemade)
- 1 cup shredded mozzarella cheese
- 1/2 cup grated Parmesan cheese
- 1/4 cup pine nuts (optional, for garnish)
- Fresh basil, chopped (for garnish)

Instructions:

Preheat your oven to 375°F (190°C). Grease a 9x13-inch baking dish.
In a large mixing bowl, combine the cooked penne pasta, shredded chicken, cherry tomatoes, and sun-dried tomatoes.
Add the pesto sauce to the bowl, tossing everything together until well coated.
Transfer the pasta mixture to the prepared baking dish, spreading it evenly.
Sprinkle shredded mozzarella cheese and grated Parmesan cheese over the top.
Bake in the preheated oven for 20-25 minutes or until the casserole is hot and bubbly, and the cheese is melted and golden brown.
While the casserole is baking, toast the pine nuts in a dry skillet over medium heat until lightly browned (if using).
Remove the casserole from the oven and let it cool for a few minutes.
Garnish with toasted pine nuts (if using) and chopped fresh basil before serving.

This Pesto Chicken and Penne Casserole is a flavorful and easy-to-make dish that combines the vibrant taste of pesto with the comforting elements of pasta and chicken. Enjoy the rich and savory flavors in every bite!

Creamy Corn and Bacon Casserole

Ingredients:

- 6 cups frozen corn kernels, thawed
- 8 slices bacon, cooked and crumbled
- 1 cup sour cream
- 1 cup mayonnaise
- 2 cups shredded cheddar cheese
- 1/2 cup grated Parmesan cheese
- 1/2 cup green onions, chopped
- 1 teaspoon garlic powder
- Salt and pepper to taste
- 1 cup crushed buttery crackers (like Ritz)
- 2 tablespoons unsalted butter, melted
- Fresh parsley, chopped (for garnish)

Instructions:

Preheat your oven to 350°F (175°C). Grease a 9x13-inch baking dish.
In a large mixing bowl, combine the thawed corn kernels and crumbled bacon.
In another bowl, mix together sour cream, mayonnaise, shredded cheddar cheese, grated Parmesan cheese, chopped green onions, garlic powder, salt, and pepper.
Add the sour cream mixture to the corn and bacon mixture, stirring until well combined.
Transfer the mixture to the prepared baking dish, spreading it evenly.
In a small bowl, mix together the crushed buttery crackers and melted butter.
Sprinkle the cracker mixture over the top of the corn mixture.
Bake in the preheated oven for 30-35 minutes or until the casserole is hot and bubbly, and the top is golden brown.
Remove from the oven and let it cool for a few minutes.
Garnish with chopped fresh parsley before serving.

This Creamy Corn and Bacon Casserole is a delightful side dish that combines the sweetness of corn with the savory goodness of bacon and a cheesy, crunchy topping. Enjoy the rich and comforting flavors!

Hawaiian Pizza Casserole

Ingredients:

- 16 ounces penne pasta, cooked according to package instructions
- 1 pound ham, diced
- 1 cup pineapple chunks, drained
- 1 red bell pepper, diced
- 1 onion, finely chopped
- 2 cups shredded mozzarella cheese
- 1/2 cup grated Parmesan cheese
- 1 can (15 ounces) pizza sauce
- 1 teaspoon dried oregano
- 1/2 teaspoon garlic powder
- Salt and pepper to taste
- Fresh basil, chopped (for garnish)

Instructions:

Preheat your oven to 375°F (190°C). Grease a 9x13-inch baking dish.
In a large mixing bowl, combine the cooked penne pasta, diced ham, pineapple chunks, diced red bell pepper, and chopped onion.
In a separate bowl, mix together shredded mozzarella cheese, grated Parmesan cheese, pizza sauce, dried oregano, garlic powder, salt, and pepper.
Add the cheese and sauce mixture to the pasta mixture, tossing everything together until well coated.
Transfer the mixture to the prepared baking dish, spreading it evenly.
Bake in the preheated oven for 20-25 minutes or until the casserole is hot and bubbly, and the cheese is melted and golden brown.
Remove from the oven and let it cool for a few minutes.
Garnish with chopped fresh basil before serving.

This Hawaiian Pizza Casserole is a fun twist on the classic pizza flavors, featuring the sweetness of pineapple and the savory goodness of ham. Enjoy the tropical and cheesy goodness in every bite!

Turkey and Cranberry Stuffing Casserole

Ingredients:

- 4 cups cooked and shredded turkey (leftover or roasted)
- 4 cups prepared stuffing
- 1 cup cranberry sauce
- 1 cup turkey gravy (homemade or store-bought)
- 1 cup shredded mozzarella cheese
- 1/2 cup chopped pecans (optional, for topping)
- Fresh parsley, chopped (for garnish)

Instructions:

Preheat your oven to 375°F (190°C). Grease a 9x13-inch baking dish.
In a large mixing bowl, combine the shredded turkey and prepared stuffing.
Spread half of the mixture evenly in the bottom of the prepared baking dish.
Drizzle half of the turkey gravy over the stuffing layer.
Spoon half of the cranberry sauce over the stuffing and gravy.
Sprinkle half of the shredded mozzarella cheese over the cranberry sauce.
Repeat the layers with the remaining stuffing mixture, turkey gravy, cranberry sauce, and mozzarella cheese.
If using, sprinkle chopped pecans over the top for added crunch.
Bake in the preheated oven for 25-30 minutes or until the casserole is hot and bubbly, and the cheese is melted and golden brown.
Remove from the oven and let it cool for a few minutes.
Garnish with chopped fresh parsley before serving.

This Turkey and Cranberry Stuffing Casserole is a wonderful way to use Thanksgiving leftovers. Enjoy the comforting combination of turkey, stuffing, cranberry sauce, and melted cheese in this flavorful casserole!

Baked Ziti with Meatballs

Ingredients:

For the Meatballs:

- 1 pound ground beef
- 1/2 pound ground pork
- 1 cup breadcrumbs
- 2/3 cup grated Parmesan cheese
- 2 large eggs
- 1/4 cup fresh parsley, chopped
- 2 cloves garlic, minced
- 1 teaspoon dried oregano
- 1 teaspoon dried basil
- Salt and pepper to taste

For the Baked Ziti:

- 1 pound ziti pasta, cooked al dente according to package instructions
- 4 cups marinara sauce
- 2 cups shredded mozzarella cheese
- 1 cup ricotta cheese
- 1/2 cup grated Parmesan cheese
- Fresh basil, chopped (for garnish)

Instructions:

Preheat your oven to 375°F (190°C). Grease a 9x13-inch baking dish.
In a large mixing bowl, combine the ground beef, ground pork, breadcrumbs, grated Parmesan cheese, eggs, chopped parsley, minced garlic, dried oregano, dried basil, salt, and pepper. Mix until well combined.
Shape the mixture into meatballs, about 1 to 1.5 inches in diameter.
In a skillet, brown the meatballs over medium heat until they are cooked through. Drain excess fat.
In a large mixing bowl, combine the cooked ziti pasta, marinara sauce, and meatballs.

In the prepared baking dish, layer half of the ziti mixture.
Dollop half of the ricotta cheese over the ziti layer, and sprinkle half of the shredded mozzarella and grated Parmesan cheese.
Repeat the layers with the remaining ziti mixture, ricotta cheese, mozzarella, and Parmesan cheese.
Cover the baking dish with aluminum foil.
Bake in the preheated oven for 25 minutes. Remove the foil and bake for an additional 10-15 minutes or until the cheese is melted and bubbly.
Remove from the oven and let it cool for a few minutes.
Garnish with chopped fresh basil before serving.

This Baked Ziti with Meatballs is a hearty and comforting dish that's perfect for family dinners or gatherings. Enjoy the combination of ziti pasta, marinara sauce, meatballs, and gooey melted cheese!

Brussels Sprouts and Bacon Gratin

Ingredients:

- 1 1/2 pounds Brussels sprouts, trimmed and halved
- 8 slices bacon, cooked and crumbled
- 2 tablespoons unsalted butter
- 2 tablespoons all-purpose flour
- 2 cups whole milk
- 1 1/2 cups shredded Gruyere cheese
- 1/2 cup grated Parmesan cheese
- Salt and pepper to taste
- 1/2 cup breadcrumbs
- Fresh parsley, chopped (for garnish)

Instructions:

Preheat your oven to 375°F (190°C). Grease a baking dish.
Bring a large pot of salted water to a boil. Add the Brussels sprouts and cook for about 5 minutes, or until they are slightly tender. Drain and set aside.
In a large skillet, melt butter over medium heat. Stir in the flour and cook for 1-2 minutes to create a roux.
Gradually whisk in the milk, stirring constantly to avoid lumps. Continue whisking until the mixture thickens.
Stir in the shredded Gruyere cheese and grated Parmesan cheese until melted and smooth. Season with salt and pepper to taste.
Add the cooked Brussels sprouts and crumbled bacon to the cheese sauce, tossing until well coated.
Transfer the mixture to the prepared baking dish, spreading it evenly.
In a small bowl, combine breadcrumbs with a little melted butter (optional).
Sprinkle the breadcrumbs over the Brussels sprouts mixture.
Bake in the preheated oven for 25-30 minutes or until the gratin is hot and bubbly, and the top is golden brown.
Remove from the oven and let it cool for a few minutes.
Garnish with chopped fresh parsley before serving.

This Brussels Sprouts and Bacon Gratin is a flavorful and cheesy side dish that's perfect for holiday dinners or any special occasion. Enjoy the combination of roasted Brussels sprouts, creamy cheese sauce, and crispy bacon!

Chicken Cordon Bleu Casserole

Ingredients:

- 4 cups cooked and shredded chicken
- 1/2 pound deli ham, chopped
- 1/2 pound Swiss cheese, shredded
- 1 cup Dijon mustard
- 1 cup mayonnaise
- 1 tablespoon lemon juice
- 1 teaspoon garlic powder
- 1/2 teaspoon onion powder
- 1/2 teaspoon dried thyme
- 1/2 teaspoon black pepper
- 1 cup breadcrumbs
- 1/4 cup melted butter
- Fresh parsley, chopped (for garnish)

Instructions:

Preheat your oven to 350°F (175°C). Grease a 9x13-inch baking dish.
In a large mixing bowl, combine the shredded chicken and chopped deli ham.
In a separate bowl, whisk together Dijon mustard, mayonnaise, lemon juice, garlic powder, onion powder, dried thyme, and black pepper.
Add the sauce mixture to the chicken and ham, tossing until well coated.
Spread the mixture evenly in the prepared baking dish.
Sprinkle shredded Swiss cheese over the top of the chicken and ham mixture.
In a small bowl, combine breadcrumbs with melted butter. Sprinkle the breadcrumb mixture over the cheese layer.
Bake in the preheated oven for 25-30 minutes or until the casserole is hot and bubbly, and the top is golden brown.
Remove from the oven and let it cool for a few minutes.
Garnish with chopped fresh parsley before serving.

This Chicken Cordon Bleu Casserole is a simplified version of the classic dish, offering all the delicious flavors of chicken, ham, Swiss cheese, and a creamy Dijon sauce in an easy-to-make casserole form. Enjoy this comforting and flavorful dish!

Butternut Squash and Sage Lasagna

Ingredients:

- 9 lasagna noodles, cooked according to package instructions
- 4 cups butternut squash, peeled, seeded, and diced
- 2 tablespoons olive oil
- Salt and pepper to taste
- 1/4 teaspoon nutmeg
- 1/2 cup unsalted butter
- 1/2 cup all-purpose flour
- 4 cups whole milk
- 1 cup grated Parmesan cheese
- 1 cup ricotta cheese
- 1 cup shredded mozzarella cheese
- 2 tablespoons fresh sage, chopped
- 1/4 cup pine nuts (optional, for garnish)

Instructions:

Preheat your oven to 375°F (190°C). Grease a 9x13-inch baking dish.

Toss the diced butternut squash with olive oil, salt, pepper, and nutmeg. Spread the squash on a baking sheet and roast in the preheated oven for about 20-25 minutes or until tender. Remove and set aside.

In a saucepan, melt the butter over medium heat. Stir in the flour to create a roux. Cook for 1-2 minutes, stirring constantly.

Gradually whisk in the milk, stirring constantly to avoid lumps. Continue whisking until the mixture thickens.

Stir in grated Parmesan cheese until melted and smooth. Season with salt and pepper to taste.

In a bowl, combine the ricotta cheese, shredded mozzarella cheese, and chopped fresh sage.

Spread a small amount of the cheese sauce in the bottom of the prepared baking dish.

Place three lasagna noodles on top of the sauce.

Layer half of the roasted butternut squash on the noodles, followed by half of the cheese mixture.

Repeat the layers with three more noodles, the remaining butternut squash, and the remaining cheese mixture.

Top with the remaining three noodles and pour the remaining cheese sauce over the top.

Bake in the preheated oven for 30-35 minutes or until the lasagna is hot and bubbly, and the top is golden brown.

If desired, sprinkle pine nuts over the top for added crunch.

Remove from the oven and let it cool for a few minutes before serving.

This Butternut Squash and Sage Lasagna is a delicious and comforting vegetarian dish that captures the rich flavors of roasted squash, sage, and creamy cheese sauce. Enjoy the layers of goodness in every bite!

Chili Cornbread Casserole

Ingredients:

For the Chili:

- 1 pound ground beef
- 1 onion, finely chopped
- 2 cloves garlic, minced
- 1 can (15 ounces) black beans, drained and rinsed
- 1 can (15 ounces) kidney beans, drained and rinsed
- 1 can (15 ounces) diced tomatoes
- 1 can (6 ounces) tomato paste
- 1 cup corn kernels (fresh, frozen, or canned)
- 1 cup beef broth
- 2 tablespoons chili powder
- 1 teaspoon ground cumin
- 1 teaspoon dried oregano
- Salt and pepper to taste

For the Cornbread Topping:

- 1 cup cornmeal
- 1 cup all-purpose flour
- 1 tablespoon sugar
- 1 tablespoon baking powder
- 1/2 teaspoon salt
- 1 cup milk
- 1/4 cup unsalted butter, melted
- 1 large egg

For Topping:

- 1 cup shredded cheddar cheese
- Fresh cilantro, chopped (for garnish)

Instructions:

Preheat your oven to 375°F (190°C). Grease a 9x13-inch baking dish.

In a large skillet, cook the ground beef over medium heat until browned. Drain excess fat.

Add chopped onion and minced garlic to the skillet. Sauté until the onions are translucent.

Stir in black beans, kidney beans, diced tomatoes, tomato paste, corn, beef broth, chili powder, ground cumin, dried oregano, salt, and pepper. Simmer for 10-15 minutes, allowing the flavors to meld.

In a bowl, whisk together cornmeal, flour, sugar, baking powder, and salt.

In another bowl, mix together milk, melted butter, and egg. Add the wet ingredients to the dry ingredients, stirring until just combined.

Pour the chili mixture into the prepared baking dish.

Spoon the cornbread batter over the top, spreading it evenly to cover the chili.

Sprinkle shredded cheddar cheese over the cornbread layer.

Bake in the preheated oven for 25-30 minutes or until the cornbread is golden brown and a toothpick inserted into the center comes out clean.

Remove from the oven and let it cool for a few minutes.

Garnish with chopped fresh cilantro before serving.

This Chili Cornbread Casserole is a comforting and hearty dish that combines the warmth of chili with the sweetness of cornbread. Enjoy the layers of flavor and textures in this delicious casserole!

Greek Moussaka

Ingredients:

For the Eggplant Layer:

- 2 large eggplants, sliced into 1/2-inch rounds
- Salt
- Olive oil for brushing

For the Meat Sauce:

- 1 1/2 pounds ground lamb or beef
- 1 onion, finely chopped
- 3 cloves garlic, minced
- 1 can (14 ounces) crushed tomatoes
- 2 tablespoons tomato paste
- 1 teaspoon dried oregano
- 1 teaspoon ground cinnamon
- Salt and pepper to taste
- 1/2 cup red wine (optional)

For the Béchamel Sauce:

- 1/2 cup unsalted butter
- 1/2 cup all-purpose flour
- 4 cups whole milk, warmed
- Salt and nutmeg to taste
- 2 large eggs, beaten
- 1 cup grated Parmesan cheese

Instructions:

Preheat your oven to 400°F (200°C).
Place the sliced eggplant on a baking sheet, sprinkle with salt, and let it sit for about 30 minutes. This helps draw out excess moisture. After 30 minutes, pat the eggplant slices dry with paper towels and brush both sides with olive oil. Arrange them on baking sheets and bake for 20-25 minutes or until golden brown. Set aside.

For the meat sauce, in a large skillet, brown the ground lamb or beef over medium heat. Add chopped onion and garlic, and cook until the onion is softened.

Stir in crushed tomatoes, tomato paste, dried oregano, ground cinnamon, salt, and pepper. If using red wine, add it to the mixture. Simmer for about 15-20 minutes, allowing the flavors to meld.

For the béchamel sauce, melt butter in a saucepan over medium heat. Whisk in the flour to create a roux. Cook for 1-2 minutes, stirring constantly.

Gradually whisk in the warm milk, continuing to whisk until the mixture thickens. Season with salt and nutmeg to taste.

In a separate bowl, beat the eggs. Gradually whisk the beaten eggs into the béchamel sauce.

Remove the saucepan from heat and stir in grated Parmesan cheese until melted and smooth.

In a greased 9x13-inch baking dish, layer half of the eggplant slices, followed by the meat sauce. Repeat with another layer of eggplant and meat sauce.

Pour the béchamel sauce over the top, spreading it evenly.

Bake in the preheated oven for 40-45 minutes or until the top is golden brown.

Remove from the oven and let it cool for a few minutes before serving.

This Greek Moussaka is a classic dish with layers of eggplant, a savory meat sauce, and a creamy béchamel topping. Enjoy the rich and comforting flavors of this traditional Greek casserole!

Philly Cheesesteak Casserole

Ingredients:

- 1 1/2 pounds thinly sliced beef sirloin or ribeye
- Salt and pepper to taste
- 2 tablespoons olive oil
- 1 onion, thinly sliced
- 1 green bell pepper, thinly sliced
- 8 ounces mushrooms, sliced
- 2 cloves garlic, minced
- 1/2 cup mayonnaise
- 1/2 cup sour cream
- 1 tablespoon Dijon mustard
- 2 cups shredded provolone cheese
- 1 cup shredded mozzarella cheese
- 1/2 cup grated Parmesan cheese
- Fresh parsley, chopped (for garnish)

Instructions:

Preheat your oven to 375°F (190°C). Grease a 9x13-inch baking dish.
Season the thinly sliced beef with salt and pepper.
In a large skillet, heat olive oil over medium-high heat. Add the sliced beef and cook until browned. Remove the beef from the skillet and set it aside.
In the same skillet, add sliced onion, sliced green bell pepper, and sliced mushrooms. Sauté until the vegetables are softened.
Add minced garlic to the skillet and sauté for an additional minute.
In a bowl, mix together mayonnaise, sour cream, and Dijon mustard.
In the prepared baking dish, layer half of the cooked beef, followed by the sautéed vegetables. Repeat with another layer of beef and vegetables.
Spread the mayonnaise mixture over the top, covering the casserole evenly.
Sprinkle shredded provolone, mozzarella, and grated Parmesan cheese over the top.
Bake in the preheated oven for 25-30 minutes or until the casserole is hot and bubbly, and the cheese is melted and golden brown.
Remove from the oven and let it cool for a few minutes.
Garnish with chopped fresh parsley before serving.

This Philly Cheesesteak Casserole is a flavorful twist on the classic sandwich, featuring tender beef, sautéed vegetables, and a cheesy, creamy topping. Enjoy the taste of a Philly cheesesteak in casserole form!

Creamy Chicken and Mushroom Casserole

Ingredients:

- 4 boneless, skinless chicken breasts
- Salt and pepper to taste
- 2 tablespoons olive oil
- 8 ounces mushrooms, sliced
- 1 onion, finely chopped
- 3 cloves garlic, minced
- 1/4 cup all-purpose flour
- 1 cup chicken broth
- 1 cup heavy cream
- 1 teaspoon dried thyme
- 1/2 teaspoon dried rosemary
- 1 cup frozen peas
- 1/2 cup grated Parmesan cheese
- 1 cup shredded mozzarella cheese
- Fresh parsley, chopped (for garnish)

Instructions:

Preheat your oven to 375°F (190°C). Grease a 9x13-inch baking dish.
Season the chicken breasts with salt and pepper.
In a large skillet, heat olive oil over medium-high heat. Add the chicken breasts and cook until browned on both sides. Remove the chicken from the skillet and set it aside.
In the same skillet, add sliced mushrooms and chopped onion. Sauté until the mushrooms release their moisture and the onion is softened.
Add minced garlic and sauté for an additional minute.
Sprinkle flour over the mushrooms and onion, stirring to combine and cook for 1-2 minutes.
Gradually whisk in chicken broth and heavy cream, stirring until the mixture thickens.
Stir in dried thyme and dried rosemary. Season with salt and pepper to taste.
Add frozen peas to the skillet and stir until they are heated through.
Slice the cooked chicken breasts and arrange them in the prepared baking dish.
Pour the creamy mushroom sauce over the chicken.

Sprinkle grated Parmesan and shredded mozzarella cheese over the top.
Bake in the preheated oven for 25-30 minutes or until the casserole is hot and bubbly, and the cheese is melted and golden brown.
Remove from the oven and let it cool for a few minutes.
Garnish with chopped fresh parsley before serving.

This Creamy Chicken and Mushroom Casserole is a comforting and flavorful dish with tender chicken, savory mushrooms, and a rich creamy sauce. Enjoy this hearty casserole for a satisfying meal!

Three-Cheese Baked Ziti

Ingredients:

- 1 pound ziti pasta
- 1 tablespoon olive oil
- 1 onion, finely chopped
- 3 cloves garlic, minced
- 1 pound ground beef or Italian sausage
- 1 can (28 ounces) crushed tomatoes
- 1 can (15 ounces) tomato sauce
- 1 teaspoon dried oregano
- 1 teaspoon dried basil
- Salt and black pepper to taste
- 2 cups ricotta cheese
- 1 cup grated Parmesan cheese
- 2 cups shredded mozzarella cheese
- 1/4 cup fresh basil, chopped (for garnish)

Instructions:

1. Preheat Oven:

    - Preheat your oven to 375°F (190°C).

2. Cook Ziti:

    - Cook the ziti pasta according to the package instructions. Drain and set aside.

3. Prepare Sauce:

    - In a large skillet, heat olive oil over medium heat. Add chopped onion and minced garlic, sautéing until softened. Add ground beef or Italian sausage, cooking until browned. Drain excess fat if necessary.

4. Add Tomatoes and Seasonings:

- Stir in crushed tomatoes, tomato sauce, dried oregano, dried basil, salt, and black pepper. Simmer the sauce for about 15-20 minutes, allowing the flavors to meld.

5. Mix Cheeses:

- In a separate bowl, combine ricotta cheese, grated Parmesan cheese, and half of the shredded mozzarella cheese.

6. Assemble Baked Ziti:

- In a large baking dish, layer half of the cooked ziti pasta, followed by half of the meat sauce and half of the cheese mixture. Repeat the layers.

7. Top with Cheese:

- Sprinkle the remaining shredded mozzarella cheese over the top.

8. Bake:

- Bake in the preheated oven for 25-30 minutes or until the cheese is melted and bubbly.

9. Garnish:

- Remove from the oven and let it rest for a few minutes. Garnish with chopped fresh basil.

10. Serve:

- Serve the Three-Cheese Baked Ziti warm and enjoy the gooey, cheesy goodness.

11. Enjoy:

- Enjoy this comforting and flavorful Three-Cheese Baked Ziti with your favorite salad or garlic bread for a satisfying meal.

Three-Cheese Baked Ziti is a classic Italian-American comfort dish that brings together ziti pasta, a hearty meat sauce, and a trio of rich cheeses. This baked ziti recipe is perfect for gatherings, family dinners, or when you're craving a comforting and cheesy pasta dish. The layers of pasta, meat sauce, and three different cheeses create a delicious and satisfying casserole that's sure to be a hit with everyone at the table.

Cabbage Roll Casserole

Ingredients:

- 1 pound ground beef
- 1 onion, finely chopped
- 2 cloves garlic, minced
- 1 cup cooked rice
- 1 can (15 ounces) tomato sauce
- 1 can (14 ounces) diced tomatoes
- 1 teaspoon dried oregano
- 1 teaspoon dried basil
- Salt and black pepper to taste
- 1 large cabbage, shredded
- 1 cup beef broth
- 1 cup shredded mozzarella cheese
- Chopped fresh parsley for garnish

Instructions:

1. Preheat Oven:

- Preheat your oven to 375°F (190°C).

2. Cook Ground Beef:

- In a large skillet, cook the ground beef over medium heat until browned. Drain excess fat if necessary.

3. Add Onion and Garlic:

- Add the chopped onion and minced garlic to the skillet with the ground beef. Sauté until the onion is softened.

4. Mix with Rice and Tomato Sauce:

- Stir in the cooked rice, tomato sauce, diced tomatoes, dried oregano, dried basil, salt, and black pepper. Let the mixture simmer for 5-7 minutes, allowing the flavors to meld.

5. Prepare Cabbage:

- In a separate pot, bring water to a boil. Add the shredded cabbage and cook for about 5 minutes until slightly softened. Drain the cabbage.

6. Layer Casserole:

- In a large baking dish, layer half of the shredded cabbage, followed by half of the ground beef mixture. Repeat the layers.

7. Pour Beef Broth:

- Pour beef broth over the layered cabbage and beef.

8. Top with Cheese:

- Sprinkle shredded mozzarella cheese over the top.

9. Bake:

- Bake in the preheated oven for 25-30 minutes or until the cheese is melted and bubbly.

10. Garnish:

- Remove from the oven and let it rest for a few minutes. Garnish with chopped fresh parsley.

11. Serve:

- Serve the Cabbage Roll Casserole warm, and enjoy the hearty and comforting flavors.

Cabbage Roll Casserole offers all the delicious flavors of traditional cabbage rolls in an easy-to-make casserole form. This recipe simplifies the classic dish by layering cooked cabbage with a seasoned ground beef and rice mixture, all topped with a savory tomato sauce and melted cheese. It's a comforting and satisfying meal that's perfect for family dinners. Enjoy the taste of cabbage rolls without the hassle of rolling each individual leaf. Serve with a side of crusty bread or a simple salad for a complete and hearty dinner.

Crab and Artichoke Casserole

Ingredients:

- 1 pound lump crabmeat, picked over for shells
- 1 can (14 ounces) artichoke hearts, drained and chopped
- 1 cup mayonnaise
- 1 cup sour cream
- 1 cup shredded Parmesan cheese
- 1 cup shredded mozzarella cheese
- 1/2 cup grated Romano cheese
- 2 cloves garlic, minced
- 1 teaspoon Worcestershire sauce
- 1 teaspoon Dijon mustard
- 1 tablespoon fresh lemon juice
- Salt and black pepper to taste
- 1/4 cup chopped fresh parsley (for garnish)
- Sliced baguette or crackers (for serving)

Instructions:

1. Preheat Oven:

- Preheat your oven to 375°F (190°C).

2. Prepare Casserole Mixture:

- In a large mixing bowl, combine lump crabmeat, chopped artichoke hearts, mayonnaise, sour cream, Parmesan cheese, mozzarella cheese, Romano cheese, minced garlic, Worcestershire sauce, Dijon mustard, fresh lemon juice, salt, and black pepper. Gently fold the ingredients until well combined.

3. Transfer to Baking Dish:

- Transfer the crab and artichoke mixture to a greased baking dish, spreading it evenly.

4. Bake:

- Bake in the preheated oven for 25-30 minutes or until the casserole is hot and bubbly, and the top is golden brown.

5. Garnish:

- Remove from the oven and garnish with chopped fresh parsley.

6. Serve:

- Serve the Crab and Artichoke Casserole hot with sliced baguette or crackers.

7. Enjoy:

- Enjoy the creamy and flavorful combination of crab and artichoke in this delicious casserole. It makes for a perfect appetizer or party dish.

Crab and Artichoke Casserole is a delectable and indulgent dish that combines the richness of lump crabmeat with the tangy flavors of artichoke hearts. This casserole is creamy, cheesy, and loaded with savory goodness. It's an excellent choice for entertaining or as an appetizer for special occasions. The blend of cheeses, along with the garlic, Worcestershire sauce, and Dijon mustard, adds layers of flavor to this irresistible dish. Serve it with sliced baguette or crackers for a delightful and satisfying experience.

Teriyaki Chicken and Rice Casserole

Ingredients:

- 2 cups cooked and shredded chicken (rotisserie chicken works well)
- 2 cups cooked white rice
- 1 cup broccoli florets, blanched
- 1 cup sliced carrots, blanched
- 1/2 cup diced red bell pepper
- 1/2 cup diced onion
- 1/2 cup teriyaki sauce
- 1/4 cup soy sauce
- 2 tablespoons honey
- 2 cloves garlic, minced
- 1 teaspoon ginger, grated
- 1 tablespoon sesame oil
- 1 tablespoon vegetable oil
- 1 cup shredded mozzarella cheese (optional)
- Green onions, chopped (for garnish)
- Sesame seeds (for garnish)

Instructions:

1. Preheat Oven:

- Preheat your oven to 375°F (190°C).

2. Prepare Casserole Mixture:

- In a large mixing bowl, combine the shredded chicken, cooked rice, blanched broccoli, blanched carrots, diced red bell pepper, and diced onion.

3. Make Teriyaki Sauce:

- In a separate bowl, whisk together teriyaki sauce, soy sauce, honey, minced garlic, grated ginger, sesame oil, and vegetable oil.

4. Combine and Mix:

- Pour the teriyaki sauce over the chicken and rice mixture. Gently toss until everything is well coated.

5. Transfer to Baking Dish:

- Transfer the mixture to a greased baking dish, spreading it evenly.

6. Add Cheese (Optional):

- If desired, sprinkle shredded mozzarella cheese over the top for an extra layer of gooey goodness.

7. Bake:

- Bake in the preheated oven for 20-25 minutes or until the casserole is heated through, and the cheese is melted and bubbly.

8. Garnish:

- Remove from the oven and garnish with chopped green onions and sesame seeds.

9. Serve:

- Serve the Teriyaki Chicken and Rice Casserole hot and enjoy the delicious flavors.

10. Enjoy:

- Enjoy this flavorful and satisfying Teriyaki Chicken and Rice Casserole for a comforting and convenient meal.

Teriyaki Chicken and Rice Casserole combines the classic Asian-inspired flavors of teriyaki with the convenience of a casserole. This dish features tender shredded chicken, fluffy white rice, and a medley of colorful vegetables, all coated in a homemade teriyaki sauce. The addition of cheese (optional) adds a delightful cheesy element to the dish. It's a perfect meal for busy weeknights or when you're craving a comforting and flavorful dinner. Customize it with your favorite vegetables and enjoy the delicious blend of teriyaki goodness.

Quinoa and Black Bean Enchilada Bake

Ingredients:

- 1 cup quinoa, rinsed and drained
- 2 cups vegetable broth or water
- 1 can (15 ounces) black beans, drained and rinsed
- 1 cup corn kernels (fresh or frozen)
- 1 cup diced bell peppers (assorted colors)
- 1 cup diced red onion
- 1 can (15 ounces) enchilada sauce
- 1 teaspoon ground cumin
- 1 teaspoon chili powder
- 1/2 teaspoon garlic powder
- Salt and black pepper to taste
- 2 cups shredded Mexican cheese blend
- Fresh cilantro, chopped (for garnish)
- Avocado slices (for garnish)
- Sour cream or Greek yogurt (optional, for serving)

Instructions:

1. Preheat Oven:

- Preheat your oven to 375°F (190°C).

2. Cook Quinoa:

- In a medium saucepan, combine quinoa and vegetable broth or water. Bring to a boil, then reduce the heat to low, cover, and simmer for 15-20 minutes or until the quinoa is cooked and the liquid is absorbed. Fluff the quinoa with a fork.

3. Prepare Vegetables:

- In a large mixing bowl, combine cooked quinoa, black beans, corn, diced bell peppers, and red onion.

4. Season and Mix:

- Add enchilada sauce, ground cumin, chili powder, garlic powder, salt, and black pepper to the quinoa and vegetable mixture. Stir until well combined.

5. Assemble Enchilada Bake:

- Transfer the mixture to a greased baking dish and spread it evenly.

6. Top with Cheese:

- Sprinkle shredded Mexican cheese blend over the top of the quinoa and vegetable mixture.

7. Bake:

- Bake in the preheated oven for 25-30 minutes or until the cheese is melted and bubbly, and the edges are golden brown.

8. Garnish:

- Remove from the oven and garnish with chopped fresh cilantro.

9. Serve:

- Serve the Quinoa and Black Bean Enchilada Bake hot, garnished with avocado slices. Optionally, serve with sour cream or Greek yogurt on the side.

10. Enjoy:

- Enjoy this wholesome and flavorful Quinoa and Black Bean Enchilada Bake for a nutritious and satisfying meal.

Quinoa and Black Bean Enchilada Bake is a wholesome and protein-packed dish that combines the goodness of quinoa, black beans, and vibrant vegetables. This recipe offers a nutritious twist on traditional enchiladas, making it a perfect option for those looking for a meatless or plant-based meal. The combination of quinoa, beans, and spices creates a flavorful and satisfying casserole that's easy to prepare and perfect for weeknight dinners. Garnish with fresh cilantro and creamy avocado slices for a finishing touch.

Pumpkin Mac and Cheese

Ingredients:

- 8 ounces elbow macaroni or pasta of choice
- 2 tablespoons unsalted butter
- 2 tablespoons all-purpose flour
- 2 cups milk (whole milk or evaporated milk for creaminess)
- 1 cup canned pumpkin puree
- 2 cups shredded sharp cheddar cheese
- 1/2 cup grated Parmesan cheese
- 1/2 teaspoon ground nutmeg
- 1/2 teaspoon dried mustard powder
- Salt and black pepper to taste
- 1/4 cup breadcrumbs (optional, for topping)
- Fresh parsley, chopped (for garnish)

Instructions:

1. Cook Pasta:

- Cook the macaroni or pasta according to the package instructions until al dente. Drain and set aside.

2. Make Cheese Sauce:

- In a large saucepan, melt the butter over medium heat. Stir in the flour to create a roux. Cook for 1-2 minutes, stirring constantly.

3. Add Milk and Pumpkin:

- Gradually whisk in the milk, making sure there are no lumps. Add the pumpkin puree and continue to whisk until well combined.

4. Melt Cheese:

- Stir in the shredded cheddar cheese and grated Parmesan cheese, allowing them to melt into the sauce.

5. Season:

- Add ground nutmeg, dried mustard powder, salt, and black pepper. Adjust seasoning to taste.

6. Combine Pasta and Sauce:

- Add the cooked pasta to the cheese sauce, tossing until the pasta is evenly coated.

7. Optional Breadcrumb Topping:

- If desired, transfer the mac and cheese to a baking dish, sprinkle breadcrumbs on top, and broil for a few minutes until the breadcrumbs are golden brown.

8. Garnish:

- Garnish with chopped fresh parsley before serving.

9. Serve:

- Serve the Pumpkin Mac and Cheese hot and enjoy the creamy and flavorful fall-inspired dish.

10. Enjoy:

- Savor the unique and comforting taste of Pumpkin Mac and Cheese, a delightful twist on the classic macaroni and cheese.

Pumpkin Mac and Cheese brings a seasonal and comforting twist to the traditional macaroni and cheese dish. The addition of pumpkin puree adds a subtle sweetness and creaminess to the cheese sauce, creating a rich and flavorful autumn-inspired meal. This dish is perfect for cozy dinners or as a side during fall gatherings. Feel free to customize the recipe to suit your taste preferences and enjoy the warm, comforting flavors of Pumpkin Mac and Cheese.

Bacon and Potato Breakfast Casserole

Ingredients:

- 6 slices bacon, cooked and crumbled
- 4 cups frozen hash browns, thawed
- 1 cup shredded cheddar cheese
- 1/2 cup diced red bell pepper
- 1/2 cup diced green bell pepper
- 1/2 cup diced onion
- 1 cup diced cooked ham or sausage (optional)
- 8 large eggs
- 1 cup milk
- 1 teaspoon Dijon mustard
- 1/2 teaspoon garlic powder
- Salt and black pepper to taste
- Fresh chives, chopped (for garnish, optional)

Instructions:

1. Preheat Oven:

- Preheat your oven to 375°F (190°C).

2. Prepare Casserole Dish:

- Grease a 9x13-inch baking dish.

3. Layer Ingredients:

- In the baking dish, layer the thawed hash browns, crumbled bacon, shredded cheddar cheese, diced red bell pepper, green bell pepper, and onion. If using ham or sausage, add it as another layer.

4. Whisk Eggs Mixture:

- In a bowl, whisk together eggs, milk, Dijon mustard, garlic powder, salt, and black pepper.

5. Pour Egg Mixture:

- Pour the egg mixture evenly over the layered ingredients in the baking dish.

6. Bake:

- Bake in the preheated oven for 35-40 minutes or until the center is set and the top is golden brown.

7. Garnish:

- Remove from the oven and let it rest for a few minutes. Garnish with chopped fresh chives if desired.

8. Serve:

- Serve the Bacon and Potato Breakfast Casserole hot, and enjoy a hearty and flavorful breakfast.

9. Enjoy:

- Delight in the delicious combination of bacon, potatoes, and eggs in this easy-to-make and satisfying breakfast casserole.

The Bacon and Potato Breakfast Casserole is a crowd-pleaser, combining the classic breakfast ingredients of bacon, potatoes, and eggs in a convenient casserole form. With the addition of bell peppers and cheese, this dish becomes a flavorful and hearty breakfast option perfect for feeding a group. Whether you're hosting brunch or preparing a comforting weekend breakfast, this casserole is sure to be a hit. Customize it by adding your favorite breakfast meats or vegetables to suit your taste preferences.

Chicken Pot Pie Casserole

Ingredients:

- 2 cups cooked and shredded chicken
- 2 cups frozen mixed vegetables (peas, carrots, corn, green beans), thawed
- 1/2 cup unsalted butter
- 1/2 cup all-purpose flour
- 1 teaspoon dried thyme
- 1 teaspoon dried rosemary
- 1 teaspoon garlic powder
- 1/2 teaspoon onion powder
- Salt and black pepper to taste
- 2 cups chicken broth
- 1 1/2 cups milk
- 1 package refrigerated crescent roll dough or puff pastry sheets
- 1 egg (for egg wash, optional)

Instructions:

1. Preheat Oven:

- Preheat your oven to 375°F (190°C).

2. Cook Chicken:

- Cook and shred the chicken if you haven't done so already.

3. Prepare Vegetables:

- If using frozen mixed vegetables, thaw them by placing them in a bowl or running them under cold water.

4. Make Sauce:

- In a large saucepan, melt the butter over medium heat. Stir in the flour, thyme, rosemary, garlic powder, onion powder, salt, and black pepper to make a roux.

5. Add Liquid:

- Gradually whisk in the chicken broth and milk, ensuring there are no lumps. Cook and stir until the mixture thickens.

6. Combine Chicken and Vegetables:

- Add the shredded chicken and mixed vegetables to the sauce, stirring until well combined. Let it simmer for a few minutes.

7. Transfer to Casserole Dish:

- Transfer the chicken and vegetable mixture to a greased 9x13-inch baking dish, spreading it evenly.

8. Top with Dough:

- Roll out the crescent roll dough or puff pastry sheets and place them on top of the chicken and vegetable mixture to form a crust. If using crescent roll dough, press the seams together.

9. Optional Egg Wash:

- If desired, whisk an egg and brush it over the top of the dough for a golden finish.

10. Bake:

- Bake in the preheated oven for 25-30 minutes or until the crust is golden brown and the filling is bubbly.

11. Serve:

- Let the Chicken Pot Pie Casserole cool for a few minutes before serving. Enjoy this comforting and classic dish!

12. Enjoy:

- Savor the homely flavors of Chicken Pot Pie Casserole, a convenient and delicious way to enjoy this timeless comfort food.

This Chicken Pot Pie Casserole brings the classic flavors of chicken pot pie in an easy-to-make casserole form. The creamy chicken and vegetable filling is topped with a golden crust made from crescent roll dough or puff pastry sheets. It's a comforting and satisfying dish perfect for family dinners or potluck gatherings. Customize the vegetables and herbs to suit your taste preferences and enjoy the heartwarming flavors of this Chicken Pot Pie Casserole.

Tex-Mex Layered Bean Dip Bake

Ingredients:

- 1 can (16 ounces) refried beans
- 1 packet taco seasoning mix
- 1 cup sour cream
- 1 cup guacamole
- 1 cup salsa
- 2 cups shredded cheddar cheese
- 1 cup diced tomatoes
- 1/2 cup sliced black olives
- 1/4 cup chopped green onions
- 1/4 cup chopped fresh cilantro
- Tortilla chips (for serving)

Instructions:

1. Preheat Oven:

- Preheat your oven to 350°F (175°C).

2. Prepare Bean Layer:

- In a mixing bowl, combine the refried beans and taco seasoning mix. Mix well.

3. Assemble Layers:

- In a baking dish or a casserole dish, spread the bean mixture as the first layer.

4. Layer Sour Cream:

- Spread the sour cream evenly over the bean layer.

5. Add Guacamole Layer:

- Spoon the guacamole over the sour cream layer and spread it gently.

6. Pour Salsa:

- Pour the salsa over the guacamole layer, spreading it evenly.

7. Sprinkle Cheese:

- Sprinkle shredded cheddar cheese over the salsa layer.

8. Add Toppings:

- Top the cheese layer with diced tomatoes, sliced black olives, chopped green onions, and chopped fresh cilantro.

9. Bake:

- Bake in the preheated oven for 15-20 minutes or until the cheese is melted and bubbly.

10. Garnish:

- Remove from the oven and let it cool for a few minutes. Garnish with additional chopped cilantro if desired.

11. Serve:

- Serve the Tex-Mex Layered Bean Dip Bake with tortilla chips for dipping.

12. Enjoy:

- Enjoy this flavorful and festive Tex-Mex dip bake at parties, gatherings, or as a tasty snack.

This Tex-Mex Layered Bean Dip Bake is a crowd-pleasing appetizer that combines the flavors of refried beans, taco seasoning, sour cream, guacamole, salsa, and cheese. The layers of colorful toppings, including tomatoes, olives, green onions, and cilantro, add freshness and vibrancy to the dish. It's a perfect party or game day snack that can be easily customized with your favorite Tex-Mex ingredients. Serve it with tortilla chips for dipping and enjoy the deliciousness of this layered bean dip bake.

Sausage and Spinach Strata

Ingredients:

- 8 slices of day-old bread, cubed
- 1 pound ground breakfast sausage
- 1 cup fresh spinach, chopped
- 1 1/2 cups shredded cheddar cheese
- 1/2 cup grated Parmesan cheese
- 1/2 cup diced onions
- 1/2 cup diced bell peppers (any color)
- 6 large eggs
- 2 1/2 cups milk
- 1 teaspoon Dijon mustard
- 1 teaspoon dried thyme
- 1/2 teaspoon garlic powder
- Salt and black pepper to taste
- Butter for greasing the baking dish

Instructions:

1. Preheat Oven:

- Preheat your oven to 350°F (175°C).

2. Cook Sausage:

- In a skillet over medium heat, cook the ground breakfast sausage until browned. Drain any excess fat.

3. Prepare Bread and Vegetables:

- In a large mixing bowl, combine the cubed bread, cooked sausage, chopped spinach, shredded cheddar cheese, grated Parmesan cheese, diced onions, and diced bell peppers.

4. Layer Mixture:

- Transfer half of the bread mixture to a buttered 9x13-inch baking dish, creating an even layer.

5. Whisk Egg Mixture:

- In a separate bowl, whisk together eggs, milk, Dijon mustard, dried thyme, garlic powder, salt, and black pepper.

6. Pour Egg Mixture:

- Pour half of the egg mixture evenly over the first layer of bread mixture.

7. Repeat Layers:

- Add the remaining bread mixture on top, followed by the rest of the egg mixture.

8. Press Down:

- Gently press down on the top layer to ensure the bread absorbs the egg mixture.

9. Refrigerate (Optional):

- If time allows, cover the baking dish and refrigerate for at least 30 minutes or overnight. This allows the bread to soak up the egg mixture.

10. Bake:

- Bake in the preheated oven for 45-50 minutes or until the strata is set and the top is golden brown.

11. Rest:

- Remove from the oven and let it rest for a few minutes before serving.

12. Serve:

- Serve the Sausage and Spinach Strata warm, and enjoy the savory and satisfying flavors.

13. Enjoy:

- Delight in the delicious combination of sausage, spinach, and cheesy goodness in this comforting strata.

This Sausage and Spinach Strata is a savory breakfast or brunch casserole that brings together the richness of sausage, the freshness of spinach, and the comforting texture of bread soaked in a flavorful egg mixture. It's a perfect dish for feeding a crowd or for a cozy family breakfast. The layers of bread, sausage, and vegetables, soaked in a seasoned egg mixture, create a delicious and hearty meal that can be prepared ahead of time for added convenience.

Lemon Blueberry French Toast Bake

Ingredients:

- 1 loaf French bread, cut into cubes
- 1 cup fresh or frozen blueberries
- 8 large eggs
- 2 cups milk
- 1/2 cup granulated sugar
- 1/4 cup unsalted butter, melted
- Zest of 1 lemon
- Juice of 1 lemon
- 1 teaspoon vanilla extract
- 1/2 teaspoon ground cinnamon
- Powdered sugar (for dusting, optional)
- Maple syrup (for serving)

Instructions:

1. Preheat Oven:

- Preheat your oven to 350°F (175°C). Grease a 9x13-inch baking dish.

2. Prepare Bread and Blueberries:

- Place half of the French bread cubes in the prepared baking dish. Sprinkle half of the blueberries over the bread cubes. Repeat with the remaining bread cubes and blueberries.

3. Whisk Egg Mixture:

- In a large bowl, whisk together eggs, milk, granulated sugar, melted butter, lemon zest, lemon juice, vanilla extract, and ground cinnamon until well combined.

4. Pour Egg Mixture:

- Pour the egg mixture evenly over the bread and blueberries in the baking dish, making sure all the bread cubes are soaked.

5. Press Down:

- Gently press down on the bread cubes with a spatula to ensure they are submerged in the egg mixture.

6. Rest:

- Allow the mixture to rest for about 15-20 minutes to let the bread absorb the liquid.

7. Bake:

- Bake in the preheated oven for 45-50 minutes or until the top is golden brown and the center is set.

8. Cool:

- Allow the Lemon Blueberry French Toast Bake to cool for a few minutes.

9. Dust with Powdered Sugar:

- Dust with powdered sugar if desired.

10. Serve:

- Cut into squares, serve warm, and drizzle with maple syrup.

11. Enjoy:

- Enjoy the delightful flavors of this Lemon Blueberry French Toast Bake, a perfect breakfast or brunch treat.

This Lemon Blueberry French Toast Bake is a delightful twist on the classic French toast casserole. The combination of tangy lemon zest, fresh blueberries, and the sweetness of the custard-soaked bread creates a flavorful and comforting breakfast dish. The convenient bake-and-serve nature of this recipe makes it ideal for busy mornings or special occasions. Dust it with powdered sugar and drizzle with maple syrup for an extra touch of sweetness. It's a crowd-pleaser that captures the essence of a leisurely brunch.

Tomato Basil Quinoa Bake

Ingredients:

- 1 cup quinoa, rinsed and drained
- 2 cups vegetable broth or water
- 1 tablespoon olive oil
- 1 onion, finely chopped
- 3 cloves garlic, minced
- 1 can (14 ounces) diced tomatoes, drained
- 1 cup cherry tomatoes, halved
- 1/2 cup sun-dried tomatoes, chopped
- 1/2 cup fresh basil, chopped
- 1 teaspoon dried oregano
- 1 teaspoon dried thyme
- Salt and black pepper to taste
- 1 1/2 cups shredded mozzarella cheese
- 1/4 cup grated Parmesan cheese
- Fresh basil leaves for garnish (optional)

Instructions:

1. Preheat Oven:

- Preheat your oven to 375°F (190°C). Grease a 9x13-inch baking dish.

2. Cook Quinoa:

- In a saucepan, combine quinoa and vegetable broth (or water). Bring to a boil, then reduce heat, cover, and simmer for 15-20 minutes or until quinoa is cooked and liquid is absorbed. Fluff with a fork.

3. Sauté Onion and Garlic:

- In a large skillet, heat olive oil over medium heat. Add finely chopped onion and sauté until softened. Add minced garlic and cook for an additional minute.

4. Combine Ingredients:

- In a large mixing bowl, combine cooked quinoa, sautéed onion and garlic, diced tomatoes, cherry tomatoes, sun-dried tomatoes, chopped basil, dried oregano, dried thyme, salt, and black pepper. Mix well.

5. Layer in Baking Dish:

- Transfer the quinoa mixture to the prepared baking dish, spreading it evenly.

6. Add Cheese:

- Sprinkle shredded mozzarella cheese and grated Parmesan cheese over the top of the quinoa mixture.

7. Bake:

- Bake in the preheated oven for 20-25 minutes or until the cheese is melted and bubbly, and the edges are golden brown.

8. Garnish:

- Remove from the oven and let it cool for a few minutes. Garnish with fresh basil leaves if desired.

9. Serve:

- Serve the Tomato Basil Quinoa Bake warm and enjoy the flavors of this wholesome and savory dish.

10. Enjoy:

- Delight in the delicious combination of quinoa, tomatoes, and basil in this flavorful and nutritious bake.

This Tomato Basil Quinoa Bake is a wholesome and flavorful dish that combines the nuttiness of quinoa with the vibrant flavors of tomatoes and basil. The addition of three types of tomatoes (diced, cherry, and sun-dried) brings a variety of textures and tastes to this dish. The melted mozzarella and Parmesan cheese on top add a savory and gooey finish. It's a versatile recipe that can be enjoyed as a main dish or a hearty side. Garnish with fresh basil leaves for a burst of freshness.

Chicken and Dumplings Casserole

Ingredients:

- 2 cups cooked and shredded chicken (rotisserie chicken works well)
- 1 cup frozen peas and carrots mix
- 1 cup frozen corn kernels
- 1/2 cup diced celery
- 1/2 cup diced onion
- 1/4 cup unsalted butter
- 1/4 cup all-purpose flour
- 1 teaspoon dried thyme
- 1 teaspoon dried rosemary
- 1 teaspoon garlic powder
- 4 cups chicken broth
- 1 cup milk
- Salt and black pepper to taste
- For Dumplings:
    - 1 cup all-purpose flour
    - 1 teaspoon baking powder
    - 1/2 teaspoon salt
    - 1/2 cup milk
    - 2 tablespoons unsalted butter, melted

Instructions:

1. Preheat Oven:

- Preheat your oven to 400°F (200°C).

2. Prepare Vegetables:

- In a large skillet, sauté the frozen peas and carrots mix, corn, diced celery, and diced onion in a bit of oil until softened. Add the shredded chicken and set aside.

3. Make Roux:

- In the same skillet, melt 1/4 cup of unsalted butter. Stir in 1/4 cup of flour, dried thyme, dried rosemary, and garlic powder until well combined.

4. Add Liquid:

- Gradually whisk in the chicken broth and milk to create a smooth sauce. Continue cooking and stirring until the mixture thickens.

5. Combine Chicken and Sauce:

- Add the sautéed vegetables and chicken mixture to the sauce, stirring until everything is well coated. Season with salt and black pepper to taste.

6. Prepare Dumplings:

- In a mixing bowl, whisk together 1 cup of flour, baking powder, and salt. Stir in the milk and melted butter until a thick batter forms.

7. Drop Dumplings:

- Drop spoonfuls of the dumpling batter onto the chicken and vegetable mixture in the skillet.

8. Bake:

- Transfer the skillet to the preheated oven and bake for 20-25 minutes or until the dumplings are golden brown and cooked through.

9. Serve:

- Serve the Chicken and Dumplings Casserole warm, and enjoy the comforting and hearty flavors.

10. Enjoy:

- Savor the deliciousness of this Chicken and Dumplings Casserole, a simplified version of the classic comfort food.

This Chicken and Dumplings Casserole is a simplified and delicious twist on the classic comfort dish. The creamy chicken and vegetable filling is topped with fluffy dumplings, creating a comforting and hearty casserole. It's a perfect option for a cozy family dinner or when you're craving a comforting dish with a touch of nostalgia. Adjust the seasoning and vegetables to suit your taste preferences, and enjoy the heartwarming flavors of this Chicken and Dumplings Casserole.

Mediterranean Eggplant and Chickpea Bake

Ingredients:

- 1 large eggplant, sliced into rounds
- 1 can (15 ounces) chickpeas, drained and rinsed
- 1 pint cherry tomatoes, halved
- 1 red bell pepper, sliced
- 1 red onion, thinly sliced
- 3 cloves garlic, minced
- 1/4 cup extra-virgin olive oil
- 1 teaspoon dried oregano
- 1 teaspoon dried thyme
- 1 teaspoon ground cumin
- Salt and black pepper to taste
- 1/2 cup crumbled feta cheese
- Fresh parsley, chopped (for garnish)
- Lemon wedges (for serving)

Instructions:

1. Preheat Oven:

- Preheat your oven to 400°F (200°C).

2. Prepare Vegetables:

- Place the eggplant slices on a baking sheet and sprinkle with salt. Let them sit for about 10-15 minutes to draw out excess moisture. Afterward, pat the eggplant dry with paper towels.

3. Assemble Bake:

- In a large mixing bowl, combine the eggplant slices, chickpeas, cherry tomatoes, red bell pepper, red onion, and minced garlic. Drizzle with extra-virgin olive oil and toss to coat the vegetables evenly.

4. Season:

- Sprinkle dried oregano, dried thyme, ground cumin, salt, and black pepper over the vegetables. Toss again to distribute the seasoning.

5. Arrange in Baking Dish:

- Transfer the seasoned vegetables to a baking dish, spreading them out evenly.

6. Bake:

- Bake in the preheated oven for 30-35 minutes or until the vegetables are tender and golden brown, stirring once or twice during the baking process.

7. Add Feta:

- Sprinkle crumbled feta cheese over the baked vegetables during the last 5-7 minutes of baking, allowing it to melt slightly.

8. Garnish:

- Remove from the oven, garnish with chopped fresh parsley, and serve with lemon wedges.

9. Serve:

- Serve the Mediterranean Eggplant and Chickpea Bake as a delicious and nutritious main dish or side.

10. Enjoy:

- Enjoy the vibrant flavors of this Mediterranean-inspired bake, filled with the goodness of eggplant, chickpeas, and a variety of flavorful vegetables.

This Mediterranean Eggplant and Chickpea Bake is a flavorful and wholesome dish that showcases the delicious combination of roasted eggplant, chickpeas, and a medley of colorful vegetables. The addition of aromatic herbs and spices enhances the Mediterranean flavors, while feta cheese provides a creamy and tangy element. It's a versatile dish that can be served as a main course or as a side dish, and it's perfect for those looking for a plant-based and nutritious meal. Serve it with lemon wedges for a burst of freshness.

Ham and Swiss Croissant Casserole

Ingredients:

- 6 large croissants, split
- 1 pound ham, thinly sliced
- 1 1/2 cups shredded Swiss cheese
- 6 large eggs
- 1 1/2 cups whole milk
- 1 teaspoon Dijon mustard
- 1/2 teaspoon onion powder
- 1/2 teaspoon garlic powder
- Salt and black pepper to taste
- 2 tablespoons unsalted butter, melted
- Fresh chives, chopped (for garnish)

Instructions:

1. Preheat Oven:

- Preheat your oven to 350°F (175°C). Grease a 9x13-inch baking dish.

2. Prepare Croissants:

- Split the croissants and place the bottom halves in the prepared baking dish.

3. Layer Ham and Cheese:

- Layer the thinly sliced ham over the croissants, followed by a generous sprinkling of shredded Swiss cheese.

4. Top with Croissant Halves:

- Place the top halves of the croissants over the ham and cheese, creating a sandwich-like arrangement.

5. Whisk Egg Mixture:

- In a mixing bowl, whisk together eggs, whole milk, Dijon mustard, onion powder, garlic powder, salt, and black pepper until well combined.

6. Pour Egg Mixture:

- Pour the egg mixture evenly over the croissants, ensuring each one is coated.

7. Press Down:

- Gently press down on the croissants to help them absorb the egg mixture.

8. Melt Butter:

- Melt the unsalted butter and brush it over the top of the croissants.

9. Bake:

- Bake in the preheated oven for 25-30 minutes or until the top is golden brown and the eggs are set.

10. Garnish:

- Remove from the oven and let it cool for a few minutes. Garnish with chopped fresh chives.

11. Serve:

- Slice the Ham and Swiss Croissant Casserole into squares and serve warm.

12. Enjoy:

- Enjoy this delicious and indulgent casserole, perfect for breakfast, brunch, or a delightful meal any time of the day.

This Ham and Swiss Croissant Casserole is a decadent and savory dish that combines the buttery flakiness of croissants with layers of thinly sliced ham and melted Swiss cheese. The egg mixture infuses the croissants with a creamy and flavorful texture, creating a satisfying and comforting casserole. It's a perfect choice for breakfast, brunch, or any occasion where you want to indulge in a delightful combination of ham, cheese, and croissants. Garnish with fresh chives for a touch of brightness.

Buffalo Cauliflower Mac and Cheese

Ingredients:

- 12 ounces elbow macaroni or your favorite pasta
- 1 head cauliflower, cut into small florets
- 3 tablespoons olive oil
- Salt and black pepper to taste
- 2 tablespoons unsalted butter
- 2 tablespoons all-purpose flour
- 2 cups whole milk
- 2 cups shredded sharp cheddar cheese
- 1/2 cup buffalo sauce (adjust to taste)
- 1/2 cup blue cheese crumbles
- 1/4 cup chopped fresh cilantro or parsley (for garnish, optional)
- 1/4 cup sliced green onions (for garnish, optional)

Instructions:

1. Preheat Oven:

- Preheat your oven to 425°F (220°C). Grease a baking sheet.

2. Roast Cauliflower:

- Toss cauliflower florets with olive oil, salt, and black pepper. Spread them in a single layer on the prepared baking sheet. Roast in the preheated oven for 20-25 minutes or until the cauliflower is golden brown and tender.

3. Cook Pasta:

- Cook the elbow macaroni or pasta according to package instructions. Drain and set aside.

4. Make Cheese Sauce:

- In a large saucepan, melt butter over medium heat. Stir in flour to create a roux. Cook for 1-2 minutes until lightly golden. Gradually whisk in the whole milk, stirring continuously to avoid lumps. Continue cooking until the mixture thickens.

5. Add Cheese:

- Reduce heat to low. Stir in shredded cheddar cheese and continue stirring until the cheese is melted and the sauce is smooth.

6. Incorporate Buffalo Sauce:

- Add buffalo sauce to the cheese sauce and mix well. Adjust the amount to your desired level of spiciness.

7. Combine Pasta and Cauliflower:

- In a large mixing bowl, combine the cooked pasta, roasted cauliflower, and buffalo cheese sauce. Mix until everything is well coated.

8. Transfer to Baking Dish:

- Transfer the mixture to a greased 9x13-inch baking dish.

9. Top with Blue Cheese:

- Sprinkle blue cheese crumbles over the top.

10. Bake:

- Bake in the preheated oven for 15-20 minutes or until the top is golden brown and the edges are bubbling.

11. Garnish:

- Remove from the oven and let it cool for a few minutes. Garnish with chopped cilantro or parsley and sliced green onions if desired.

12. Serve:

- Serve the Buffalo Cauliflower Mac and Cheese hot and enjoy the spicy and cheesy goodness.

13. Enjoy:

- Delight in the bold flavors of buffalo cauliflower combined with creamy mac and cheese for a delicious and satisfying meal.

This Buffalo Cauliflower Mac and Cheese is a flavorful twist on the classic comfort dish, adding a spicy kick with buffalo sauce and the unique taste of roasted cauliflower. The creamy cheese sauce, blended with the tangy buffalo flavor, creates a comforting and indulgent dish. The blue cheese crumbles on top add a delightful touch of richness. Garnish with fresh cilantro or parsley and sliced green onions for added freshness and color. It's a perfect dish for those who enjoy a bit of heat and a creative spin on traditional mac and cheese.

Cornbread and Sausage Stuffing Casserole

Ingredients:

- 1 pound ground sausage (pork or turkey)
- 1 large onion, finely chopped
- 3 celery ribs, finely chopped
- 2 cloves garlic, minced
- 8 cups cornbread, cubed and dried
- 1 cup chicken broth
- 1/2 cup unsalted butter, melted
- 2 teaspoons poultry seasoning
- 1 teaspoon dried sage
- 1/2 teaspoon dried thyme
- Salt and black pepper to taste
- Fresh parsley, chopped (for garnish, optional)

Instructions:

1. Preheat Oven:

- Preheat your oven to 350°F (175°C). Grease a 9x13-inch baking dish.

2. Cook Sausage:

- In a skillet over medium heat, cook the ground sausage until browned. Remove any excess fat.

3. Sauté Vegetables:

- In the same skillet, sauté the chopped onion, celery, and minced garlic until softened.

4. Mix Cornbread and Sausage:

- In a large mixing bowl, combine the cubed and dried cornbread with the cooked sausage and sautéed vegetables.

5. Prepare Seasonings:

- In a separate bowl, whisk together chicken broth, melted butter, poultry seasoning, dried sage, dried thyme, salt, and black pepper.

6. Combine Wet and Dry Ingredients:

- Pour the seasoned chicken broth mixture over the cornbread and sausage mixture. Gently toss until everything is evenly coated.

7. Transfer to Baking Dish:

- Transfer the stuffing mixture to the prepared baking dish, spreading it out evenly.

8. Bake:

- Bake in the preheated oven for 25-30 minutes or until the top is golden brown and the edges are crispy.

9. Garnish:

- Remove from the oven and let it cool for a few minutes. Garnish with chopped fresh parsley if desired.

10. Serve:

- Serve the Cornbread and Sausage Stuffing Casserole as a delicious side dish for your holiday feast or any meal.

11. Enjoy:

- Enjoy the comforting and savory flavors of this casserole, combining the richness of sausage with the classic taste of cornbread stuffing.

This Cornbread and Sausage Stuffing Casserole is a delightful twist on traditional stuffing, combining the savory goodness of ground sausage with the comforting flavors of cornbread. The blend of herbs and seasonings adds depth to the dish, making it a perfect side for your holiday gatherings or any hearty meal. The crispy top and moist interior create a satisfying texture, and the addition of fresh parsley adds a burst of color and freshness. Serve this casserole alongside your favorite main dishes for a delicious and memorable dining experience.